TOY
SOLDIERS

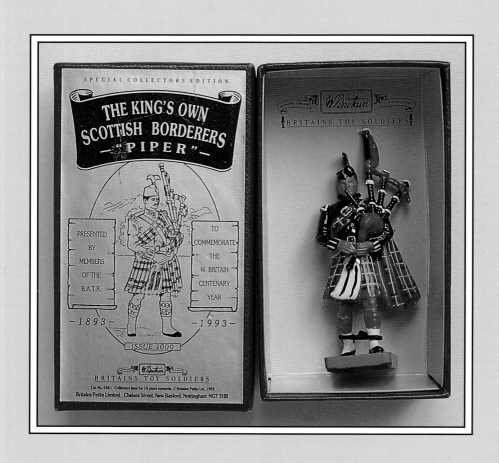

TOY SOLDIERS

THE COLLECTOR'S GUIDE TO IDENTIFYING, BUYING AND ENJOYING TOY SOLDIERS

Norman Joplin

THE APPLE PRESS

DEDICATION

To Sheila, my wife, who continued to support me throughout and
for her encouragement when the going got tough.

A QUINTET BOOK

Published by The Apple Press
6 Blundell Street
London N7 9BH

ISBN 1-85076-533-2

This book was designed and produced by
Quintet Publishing Limited
6 Blundell Street
London N7 9BH

Creative Director: Richard Dewing
Designer: Peter Laws
Project Editor: Helen Denholm
Editor: Lydia Darbyshire
Photographer: Ian Howes

ACKNOWLEDGEMENTS
The author would like to thank the following people
without whom it would not have been possible to
complete this book:
Britains Petite Limited, Brian Carrick, Kim Fitzgerald,
Adrian Little, Don Pielin, John Waterworth, Brian Wicks
and Rob Wilson, who all provided figures for photography
or supplied valuable information; and Angela Haigh, who
typed the manuscript.

Typeset in Great Britain by
Central Southern Typesetters, Eastbourne
Manufactured in Singapore by Eray Scan Pte Ltd
Printed in China by Leefung-Asco Printers Limited

CONTENTS

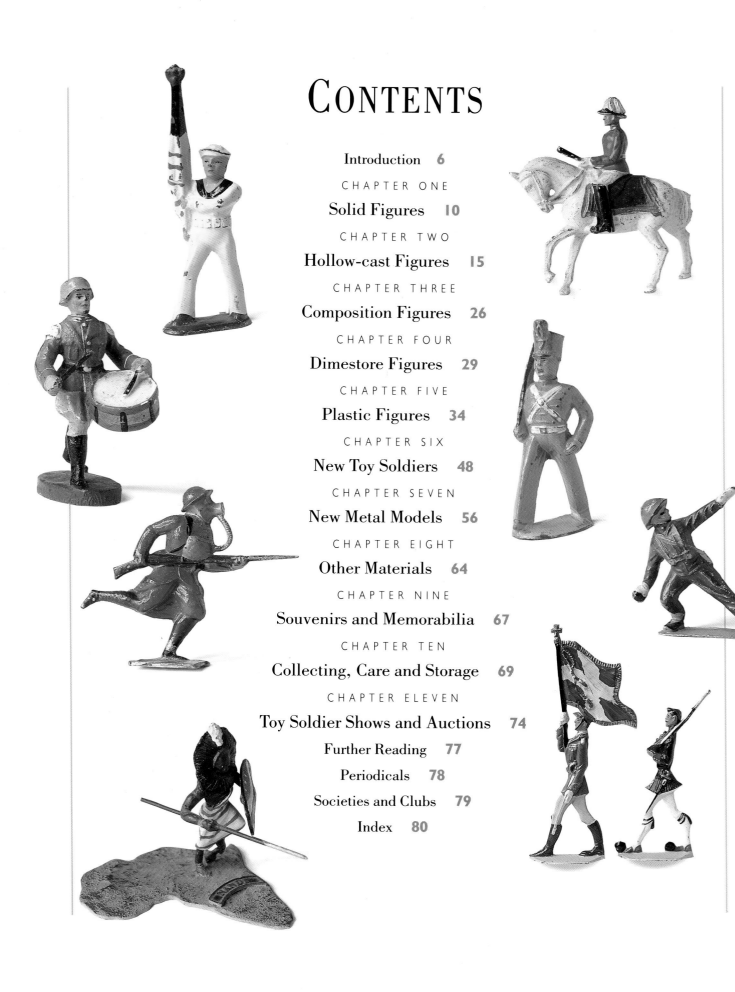

Introduction   6

CHAPTER ONE

Solid Figures   10

CHAPTER TWO

Hollow-cast Figures   15

CHAPTER THREE

Composition Figures   26

CHAPTER FOUR

Dimestore Figures   29

CHAPTER FIVE

Plastic Figures   34

CHAPTER SIX

New Toy Soldiers   48

CHAPTER SEVEN

New Metal Models   56

CHAPTER EIGHT

Other Materials   64

CHAPTER NINE

Souvenirs and Memorabilia   67

CHAPTER TEN

Collecting, Care and Storage   69

CHAPTER ELEVEN

Toy Soldier Shows and Auctions   74

Further Reading   77

Periodicals   78

Societies and Clubs   79

Index   80

INTRODUCTION

The practice of making miniature representations of soldiers can be traced back to Ancient Egyptian times, for the first small warrior-like figures were discovered in the tombs of the Pharaohs, where they were probably placed as part of religious ceremonies. Examples of solid figures from Roman times can be seen in the British Museum, London, and these are thought to have been playthings. The discovery at Xian in China of a full-size terracotta army bears testimony to the compulsion for real-life military examples to be reproduced.

Toy soldiers were for children. At first they were available in limited numbers and so were expensive and tended to be bought for the children of the nobility. Later, as the manufacturing process became more sophisticated, more soldiers at cheaper prices became available for all children to enjoy. By the late 19th century many a Victorian Christmas tree would be surrounded by all manner of toys, and for boys boxes of toy soldiers became a must. Some of the first toy soldiers of a commercial nature were flat, solid and made of lead in Nuremberg in Germany during the mid-

LEFT

Flat figures made in Austria or Germany were very popular on the continent of Europe and are still avidly collected in these countries today, although they are less popular elsewhere in the world. The flats shown here, which are probably Austrian, date from c.1930 and depict soldiers from various American War of Independence troops. They are 30mm (1¼in) high. The scope for producing figures in this flat form is immense, and many millions must have been produced. Flats are ideal for exhibitions when large numbers are needed because they take up much less room than full-size, fully rounded figures. Museums, for example, use flats when they mount displays of battles.

BELOW
Tradition of London manufactured this solid military miniature of an officer from the Zulu War in 1970. The level of detail and intricate paint finish make this more of a model soldier than a toy. It is 54mm (2¼in) high.

ABOVE

Solid figures produced by Holger Eriksson who designed for his own Authenticast range and also for the American firm of Comet. The kneeling figure to the right is a Comet item while the others and the box are Authenticast. They are 54mm (2¼in) high.

RIGHT

This hollow-cast British Army infantryman in a World War I uniform is depicted in a casual pose that is not often adopted by manufacturers. It is an unusual figure, by an unidentified UK manufacturer, standing 65mm (2½in) high and probably dating from c.1920.

18th century. Heinrichsen was one of the major manufacturers. Semi-flat soldiers were also produced in Germany at this time. The toy soldier as we know it today probably evolved from the solid, fully rounded figures produced in France as early as 1790. At first the rounded solid lead toy soldiers were from Germany or France, countries with a long-standing toy manufacturing tradition, but soon this was to change. The invention of the hollow-cast lead soldier, devised in the UK by the aptly named William Britain Junior in 1893, began the toy soldier revolution, and continental toy soldiers soon fell from favour with the patriotic UK consumer. Many firms imitated William Britain Junior's process, and the addition of farms and zoos, boy scouts and cowboys and Indians to their ranges allowed UK manufacturers to capture the lion's share of the toy soldier market from their continental counterparts.

Production continued throughout Europe up to and during World War I, with minor attempts being made to produce toy soldiers in the USA. By World War II the US market had become self-sufficient with ranges of slush- or hollow-cast toy soldiers, which were available through the "five and dime" stores. Later, these

BELOW AND RIGHT
Before the US dimestore soldier was perfected, 54mm (2¼in) figures were produced by a few companies. The American Soldier Company made the Victorian-style sailor in a straw hat in the late 1920s, while the US infantry figure was manufactured during the early 1950s by Lincoln Logs.

RIGHT
Alymer of Spain made this 60mm (2⅜in) high figure of a nurse in a cape. The company was best known for its range of heraldic knights, but it made a number of other ranges, including personality figures and world leaders such as Mao Tse-tung, Hitler and several American Presidents.

RIGHT
Despite its name, Playwood Plastics used a composition material including wood flour. The kneeling, firing figure, 75mm (3in) high, was probably produced in 1942 in an attempt to keep toy soldier production going while lead was not available. Playwood figures would have been available in dimestores.

figures were given the nickname "dimestore", and the name has stuck and is now synonymous with US toy soldiers.

Most production ceased during World War II; up to this time Germany, France and Italy had continued to produce and issue solid toy soldiers, while British manufacturers continued with the more economical method of hollow casting. Germany had started producing composition figures during the mid-1930s by combining a mixture of sawdust, pumice powder and glue, sculptured around a wire frame or armature. The majority of these German soldiers were troops of the Third Reich. After World War II the production of lead figures resumed, but experiments were already taking place with plastic, and by the early 1950s many UK and continental companies were turning to the plastic injection moulding system. The manufacture of hollow-cast lead figures in the UK ceased in 1966 when legislation prohibited the sale of items which contained lead paint. Lead military miniatures of a

RIGHT

Britains' Deetail figures including a cowboy, a Mexican, and two American Indians, all 54mm (2¼in) high. They are pictured with a Herald totem pole and were made in 1979.

LEFT

This dimestore World War II US infantryman with the Stars and Stripes has a removable tin helmet. The figure, which is 75mm (3in) high, was made by Barclay.

RIGHT

Greenwood and Ball made this solid-cast Highland officer, 54mm (2¼in) high, c.1953 as part of a range of military miniatures. The paintwork is highly detailed. Greenwood, who produced solids before World War II, employed Miss Ball to paint for him during the 1950s and these figures were available in a limited number of militaria shops in the London area during that period.

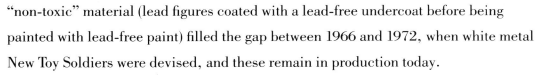

"non-toxic" material (lead figures coated with a lead-free undercoat before being painted with lead-free paint) filled the gap between 1966 and 1972, when white metal New Toy Soldiers were devised, and these remain in production today.

In common with all fields of collecting it is only when items become unavailable that the fascination to accumulate either for pleasure or investment becomes paramount. So it is with toy soldiers. Collecting them started to become fashionable in the early 1960s as the hollow-cast and other lead soldiers were being discontinued. The more difficult objects are to find, the more desirable they are to the collector. Some collectors are trying to relive the days of childhood by acquiring the long lost Christmas gifts of years gone by; others, perhaps from a military background, gain pleasure in forming parades or battlegrounds with toy soldiers. Whatever the reason, the hobby is now more for adults than children, although it permits the adult to recapture a small part of his or her childhood.

CHAPTER ONE

SOLID FIGURES

Solid toy soldiers were first produced as a commercial venture as long ago as 1760. At first they were flat, but quickly the desire for more realistic figures took hold and the French firm of Lucotte produced solid, fully rounded toy soldiers depicting units of the French Imperial Army. These were the first toy soldiers intended to represent the real thing. The Napoleonic wars provided scope for Lucotte to issue a wide range of troops from the various conflicts. Lucotte toy soldiers may be easily identified by the Imperial-bee, which is stamped on the underside of the base of each figure. Lucotte toy soldiers are rare today, but a mirrored display case at Blenheim Palace, Oxfordshire, contains a unique array of Napoleonic troops by Lucotte, and it is a worthwhile starting point for aspiring collectors. The solid method of manufacture involved a two-piece mould that was filled with molten lead. After the lead had cooled the figure was extracted. The continental manufacturers produced heads from separate moulds that were then plugged into the body of the figure.

By 1825 CBG Mignot of Paris had taken over the firm of Lucotte, and began to introduce many new ranges of toy soldiers, at first from various periods of French history, but later diversifying into armies of the world. They produced almost all of the French and French-Colonial regiments together with

ABOVE

The French company Mignot made these two Roman figures, both of which were in production for many years. These examples were probably issued during the 1970s from moulds made 60 years earlier. The solid figures are 58mm (2⅓in) high.

representative figures from many of the world's other armies, particularly those in conflict with the French. Those involved in the Napoleonic campaigns were popular subjects. They were hand-painted and fairly accurate in uniform detail. Mignot was in existence until the early 1990s, but it is believed to have fallen victim to the economic recession of the 1980s and 1990s.

Germany runs a close second to France in the production of solid-cast toy soldiers. Georg Heyde of Dresden produced toy soldiers from 1870 to 1944, when the factory was destroyed by Allied bombing raids. Heyde figures come in a range of sizes but most are 45mm (1¾in) in size, unlike the 54mm (2¼in) figures of Lucotte and Mignot, which has become the standard and recognized size of a toy soldier. Toy soldiers are measured from the top of the base to the forehead, which means that thick bases or tall headgear do not affect the scale.

Like Mignot figures, Heyde toy soldiers have plug-in heads, which means that a whole variety of regiments could be created by putting different heads on different torsos. The Heyde range featured some massive display sets. These included soldiers in

ABOVE
Heyde of Germany made this unusual large-size figure of a British lancer in the 1920s. The horse's saddle-cloth and rider are cast as individual pieces and are detachable. This rare item, some 200mm (8in) high, would command a high price at auction.

RIGHT
The German manufacturer Georg Heyde made this solid Austrian infantryman, advancing with fixed bayonet, c.1930. Like most Heyde figures, the head plugs into the body, and it is just under 54mm (2¼in) high.

LEFT
Lead flats are usually associated with Austria or Germany. However, these 30mm (1¼in) high figures were probably made in the UK in the 1920s. They were available in cigarette packets from Greys Cigarette Co.

ABOVE
Treasure Chest, a US manufacturer of solid soldiers, produces a range depicting the American Civil War of which this wounded Confederate soldier, standing 54mm (2¼in) high, is part.

ABOVE
A solid-cast British infantry figure on a camel is similar in style to some of the German semi-round figures. It is, in fact, a modern reproduction, 60mm (2⅜in) high, based on a typical 1930s design.

ABOVE
Figur of Italy was responsible for the manufacture of figures 60mm (2⅜in) high of the Vatican Guard. These figures have plug-in heads, similar to those made in France by Mignot and in Germany by Heyde. The 54mm (2¼in) high Sturmabteilung German figure (top), with a tinplate swastika flag, and the carabiniere are also solid figures, but the manufacturers are unknown. All were produced before World War II.

action poses (firing, charging, etc.) and people in domestic poses (cooks, nurses, doctors and so on), together with additions like encampments of tents and field hospitals, which increased the play value for children. Mignot preferred to remain with conventional marching or ceremonial troops.

German and French solid toy soldiers were exported in vast quantities to the UK and to America, and although some US manufacturers attempted to imitate the solid process in the late 19th century, these attempts were largely unsuccessful. In the UK W.Y. Carman, a founder member of the British Model Soldier Society, introduced a range of solid figures, many depicting the uniforms of British regiments from history. This short-lived venture, which started in the mid-1930s, did not continue after World War II.

CONNOISSEUR FIGURES

Solid toy soldiers, made not as children's toys but as military miniatures, were available after the War from exclusive shops such as Hummel and Tradition in central London. In the main they were the standard 54mm (2¼in) size. However, larger sizes were made, sometimes in kit form, ready for the collector to assemble and paint. They were designed for adults who were interested in precise uniform detail. The development of these figures was the

RIGHT

At around the time of the 1953 Coronation, Russell Gamage, famous for the manufacture of toy trains, produced a number of figures depicting the event. This 1815 British officer which is 54mm (2¼in) high was also made and sold alongside the others. It is more a military miniature than a toy, and although it would have been an expensive purchase at the time, it would not have gained much in value since.

ABOVE

This Heyde or Heyde-like mounted guardsman is unusual in that the figure is solid while the horse is semi-round. A hole in the saddle accommodates the plug that is attached to the man, in the same way as plug heads were attached to bodies. The figure is 60mm (2⅜in) high and was made c.1930.

ABOVE

Greenwood and Ball produced this example of the model soldier-style of intricately painted figure. This officer, depicted reading orders, is solid cast and would have been made in the late 1960s during the transitional period between the end of hollow-cast manufacture and the appearance of New Toy Soldiers. It is 54mm (2¼in) high.

ABOVE

Charles Stadden is known for the range of military miniatures he produced. This 1815 volunteer, made in 1973, is easily identifiable as a Stadden product by the thin, tinplate base and the paper label describing the soldier. It is 54mm (2¼in) high.

RIGHT

The US Honor Guard is an unusual subject, here portrayed by Stadden and sold through the former London Collector's Shop, which was owned by Norman Newton in the 1950s and 1960s. Solid and rather toy-like, it was an experiment in providing military miniature figures painted as toys. It is 54mm (2¼in) high.

RIGHT
Charles Stadden made solid 30mm (1¼in) high military miniatures in the 1950s. This group of Napoleon and his generals at a map table, made during the mid-1960s, would have been available in exclusive toy soldier shops or military museums at the time.

start of the distinction between model soldiers produced for adults as opposed to toys made for children. Two of the best-known manufacturers producing these figures between 1950 and 1970 were Charles Stadden and Rose Miniatures. This area of collecting, which was given the all-embracing nickname of "connoisseur figures", enabled the purchaser with rather more money than the average child to buy intricate reproductions of regimental uniforms in the form of miniature figures.

The interest in connoisseur or military miniatures continued in France, where these items could be purchased in exclusive shops near the Musée de l'Armée, while New York's Madison Avenue and Polk's Hobby Stores provided the US collector with the opportunity to purchase military miniatures.

Swedish designer Holger Eriksson designed the Authenticast range which was manufactured in Ireland for the US company, Comet. He also designed some 30mm (1¼in) troops for Swedish African Engineers, a company based in South Africa. These two companies provided the opportunity for collectors worldwide to obtain these solid but expensive playthings. Figur of Italy and Alymer of Spain made similar items which were for sale only in the European market.

These connoisseur figures do not form a major part of the current toy soldier collecting scene but they are interesting in the sense that they were the first miniature soldiers made specifically for adult consumption.

·········· N E W   D E V E L O P M E N T S ··········

The recent collapse of the USSR brought to light a number of Russian toy soldier companies that use the traditional solid-cast method. The Anglo-Russian Toy Soldier Company and Insel are but two companies who are making huge efforts to break into the worldwide toy soldier market. It remains to be seen whether these items will ever be collectible.

ABOVE
Manufacturers in eastern Europe did not have many opportunities to break into the toy or toy soldier retail markets. These solid, rather crude figures were probably made in the USSR c.1968 and they are 52mm (2⅛in) high.

RIGHT
Insel of Moscow is one of a number of companies to have started to produce solid toy soldiers since the demise of communism. The 1812 soldier shown here is hand-painted and was presented as a gift to the author by the president of the company in 1993. The figure is 60mm (2⅜in) high.

CHAPTER TWO

HOLLOW-CAST FIGURES

U ntil 1893 toy soldiers had been made of lead that was cast into solid figures, and although the process was fairly expensive, it was the only one available. William Britain, a UK toy manufacturer, had been producing mechanical toys for several years before his son, William Britain Jr, conceived and perfected the hollow-cast method of production. Like most new ideas, the process was simple, but it revolutionized toy soldier production, which had hitherto been dominated by solid figures made in France and Germany.

The hollow-cast method enabled several figures to be cast from one quota of lead. Molten lead was poured into a cold mould, which had an air hole and an escape route for excess lead, and the caster, with a deft movement of the wrist, swirled the molten metal around the mould and quickly poured the excess lead through the hole in the mould. The lead discarded in this way was used again, so that several toy soldiers could be cast. The soldier was, in fact, nothing more than a shell, empty and light to the touch. Quality controllers checked the weight, and overweight soldiers were put back into the melting-pot so that the lead could be reused. The figure was extracted from the mould with pliers before more lead was poured in to make another soldier. The days of the solid toy soldier were numbered, because the cost of a hollow-cast toy was a

ABOVE
This Britains Ltd mounted Life Guard trumpeter dates from 1959 and was available only in the Picture Pack series, which enabled collectors to purchase an individual figure in a box rather than having to buy a boxed set of five. The figure stands 90mm (3½in) high.

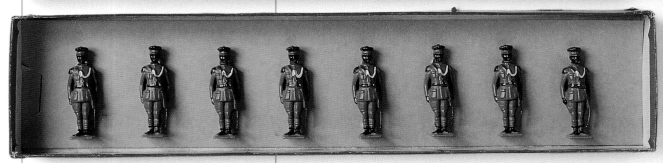

Armies of the World labels were used on Britains boxes before World War II. This set, which contains examples of the Emperor of Ethiopia's Bodyguard, is much sought after. The soldiers are still tied into the box with thread, making the set even more desirable. These soldiers are 54mm (2¼in) high.

LEFT

Crescent was a prolific UK manufacturer of toy soldiers in the 1950s. The company made many examples of guardsmen, 54mm (2¼in) high, for the cheaper end of the retail market, and because they were made in such vast numbers, they have little value, although they are of interest as typical toy soldiers of their time.

fraction of that of a solid figure. The amount of lead needed for a hollow-cast figure was about one-third of that needed for its solid equivalent.

BRITAINS LTD

The first hollow-cast figure produced by William Britain was a set of mounted Life Guards, which appeared in 1893 and was designated catalogue item no. 1. In keeping with the regiment's position within the British Army, item no. 2, which also appeared in 1893, was a set of Horse Guards. Both these sets contained five figures. The first set of infantry figures (set no. 11) was also brought out in 1893. So began a long line of issues depicting regiments of the British Army.

The toy soldiers made by William Britain were an instant success with children, partly because of the lower cost and partly because of the attractive red boxes in which the soldiers were packed. Colourful labels added to the attraction, and patriotic families preferred to purchase a toy soldier with *Made In England* on the box. Britain approached Arthur Gamage, the owner of the large department store in Holborn, London, and persuaded him to purchase and feature only Britains soldiers in the store's Christmas toy department displays. These displays were massive, and the subsequent marketing of Britains toy soldiers virtually brought an end to continental imports.

Britains production increased over the next few years. Arms were cast in individual moulds, thus making the arms movable, and the company's advertisements stressed this development and made the point that it increased the play value for children. The advertisement also made much of the fact that the company's toy soldiers were hand-painted using British labour.

In addition to British regiments, Britains produced regiments from other countries, some reflecting the conflicts of the day, with the name Armies of the World on the box labels. Production continued to increase up to and during World War I. As with all toy soldiers, the original packaging adds to the value and collectors will pay a premium for soldiers still contained within their boxes.

The success of Britains toy soldiers brought problems. Many smaller manufacturers emerged just after the turn of the century in north London near to the Britains factory – A. Fry, C.D. Abel & Co. and Hanks Brothers, for example, saw that the hollow-cast toy soldier was a money-spinner. Many of the employees or owners of these smaller companies had learnt the hollow-casting method when they had been employed by Britains, and they decided to market their own versions of the hollow-cast figures. Many of these were flagrant copies of Britains toy soldiers, and in some cases they were sold more cheaply than their competitor's products. Britains decided that it would have to stop this practice, and it carried out several successful prosecutions, forcing these smaller companies to cease copying. The firms of Mudie and Davies could not withstand these injunctions, and they were forced out of business. Fry, Hanks and Abel together with several others regrouped, however, and came up with their own individual designs and continued in business. This piracy taught Britains a valuable lesson, and the company started to apply copyright to its figures, at first by means of a small paper sticker on the underside of the soldier's base, a method which began in 1900, and then, as the moulds wore out, by having the tradename, date and copyright stamped on the bases of the figures or bellies of horses for mounted troops. The earlier paper stickers can help to date soldiers and can also add to their value.

The Britains factory assisted the war effort during World War I by producing various lead components related to munitions. This did not stop the production of toy soldiers, although it slowed down as the war progressed. The company had issued its first examples

ABOVE
Early hollow-cast manufacturers in the UK were responsible for producing many figures that resembled Britains items. Fry and Hanks, however, after being prosecuted for piracy, did produce their own unique moulds. The khaki figure (bottom) represents a Canadian soldier and was sold by Fry in boxes marked *Sons of the Empire*. The guardsman at the trail (top) was made by Hanks Brothers. Note the unusually long rifle. Both figures are 54mm (2¼in) high.

This Britains self-propelled gun, mounted on a Centurion tank body, was a very ambitious product, which was made c.1955. It is seen here in its original corrugated cardboard box. It is 300mm (12in) long and 100mm (4in) high.

Britains 4.7 naval gun remained in production from the early 1900s until the mid-1970s. It fired matchsticks and was responsible for wounding many a toy soldier during its lifetime. This boxed example is now a collector's item. It stands 54mm (2¼in) high and is 23cm (9in) long.

of khaki troops in 1899. In 1900 City Imperial Volunteers and Imperial Yeomanry Regiments were issued in their distinctive khaki uniforms.

Britains established an office in Paris in 1905 and this resulted in the creation of new figures, many of which were based on the uniforms of French units. Gun teams and ambulance wagons with troops dressed in the khaki uniforms of World War I troops were added in 1916. As khaki uniforms changed leading up to World War II, Britains updated their models to reflect this. During World War I the UK factory scaled down its production but the French

ABOVE
British Army-style labels were used by Britains for khaki troops. These infantry in battledress with gas masks are among the more often found items in the range. They are 54mm (2¼in) high.

ABOVE
This 54mm (2¼in) high British cannon by Britains had a varied history. It was used with hollow-cast US Civil War artillerymen in the 1950s, as a Waterloo cannon in the 1960s and finally with plastic Eyes Right and Herald US Civil War Soldiers until the early 1980s.

office seemed to maintain its momentum by constantly issuing figures which are now a rare find for a collector.

After World War I horse-drawn vehicles, cowboys and Indians, boy scouts and artillery pieces were introduced to the range. Large quantities of sets representing famous regiments, both British and foreign, were produced up until World War II, when production was stopped and the factory was turned over to munitions work as part of the war effort. One of the final major achievements prior to World War II was the design and issue of the State Coach in time for the 1937 Coronation. This magnificent item was a masterpiece of design, and it found its way, together with models of King George VI and Queen Elizabeth, into many homes as a treasured possession and a souvenir of the occasion to be proudly displayed in china cabinets or on the mantelpiece.

After World War II Britains was keen to start production of toy soldiers again. However, government restrictions on the availability of lead proved to be most frustrating. Soldiers from many of the Balkan countries and some European soldiers were deleted. Britains even went to the extent of advertising that it was ready to restart production, and it urged the buying public to write to their Members of Parliament to have government legislation relaxed to release lead for toy manufacture. The process was slow and at first only partially relaxed, so that toys could be made for export only to bolster the ailing post-war economy. Large amounts of Britains soldiers were, therefore, destined for the USA, and it

was not until the late 1940s that home production was brought back to its pre-war strength. It was perhaps during this time that experiments were started into plastic production, the next revolutionary process which was to take the toy soldier market by storm. This development however was still many years away.

Regiments of All Nations which contained foreign Commonwealth and Empire troops of the post-war period was the name chosen to replace Armies of the World, and many new items appeared in Britains sales catalogues. Many of the older foreign regiment lines were discontinued as the disappearance of these nations during the war meant that representative toy soldiers of their armies were no longer viable sales lines.

Probably the most significant post-war event was the Coronation of Queen Elizabeth II. The State Coach was revived and footmen, grooms and Yeomen of the Guard were added, along with many new issues of units of the British and Empire forces that were to march in the Coronation Procession. Britains made "special" figures for inclusion in a mechanical procession of toy soldiers that

ABOVE
Regiments of All Nations was the title adopted by Britains after World War II. This box contains a double row of infantry of the line. The blue slip of paper was a packer's reference, included to enable the customer to return damaged or unsatisfactory sets.

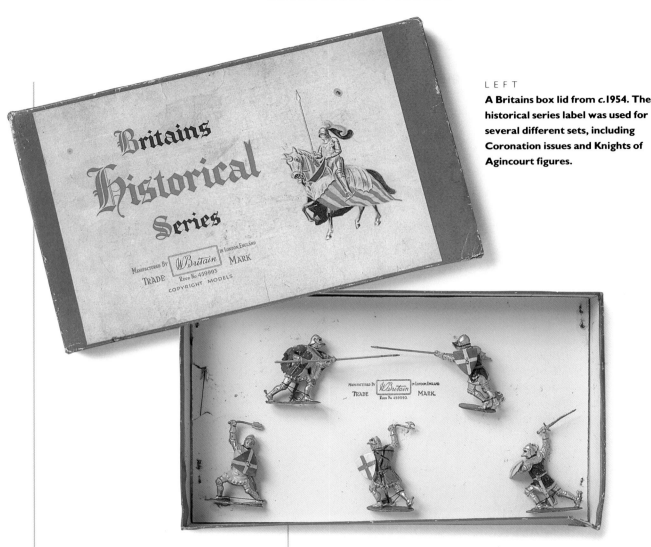

**A Britains box lid from c.1954. The
historical series label was used for
several different sets, including
Coronation issues and Knights of
Agincourt figures.**

ABOVE
**Britains Knights of Agincourt,
which were designed by Roy
Selwyn Smith, were available in
boxed sets. The knights were a
welcome addition to the range of
historical figures and were
something of a departure from the
usual run of figures, being in action
poses. They were 54mm (2¼in)
high.**

adorned the windows of Lyons Corner House at Marble Arch in
London in 1953.

In 1954, Roy Selwyn Smith (previously an employee of M.
Zang at Herald) was employed as a designer and this resulted in –
among other things – a series of action figures entitled Knights of
Agincourt. These superb figures were a departure from the
somewhat rigid toy soldiers previously produced.

Toy soldiers in individual boxes and named Picture Packs were
issued in 1959. They were mainly taken from existing sets and just
packaged separately, although a few new figures were designed to
increase the range. These are rare and are now much sought after
by collectors. The series lasted for six years. The design of some
boxed sets changed shortly after this and cellophane windows
appeared on the boxes. Government regulations governing the lead
content in children's toys were introduced in 1967, and Britains
toy soldier production was scaled down to conform. In 1966
hollow-cast toy soldiers were deleted from Britains catalogues.

ABOVE
John Hill & Co. of London made this hollow-cast figure of an airman in a donkey jacket before World War II. It is one of a range issued by Hill during the 1930s and is typical of the type of figures that were available from Woolworths. It is 54mm (2¼in) high.

ABOVE
John Hill & Co. made this nurse, 54mm (2¼in) high, both before and after World War II as part of its hollow-cast range. Many companies made examples of female military figures, and some collectors specialize in this group of figures.

ABOVE
John Hill & Co. produced this 90mm (3½in) high mounted Royal Scots Grey standard bearer both before and after World War II. The lead flag was replaced by a paper version when lead was in short supply after 1945.

OTHER HOLLOW-CAST MANUFACTURERS

Over the years since 1893 more than 100 UK firms produced hollow-cast toy soldiers and figures. Before 1914 John Hill, Fry, Hanks, Reka and BMC were perhaps the most prolific. John Hill & Co., sometimes known as Johillco, was second in size to Britains and Britains' main rival. The founder of the company, George Wood, had been an employee of Britains, and he had learnt his hollow-casting skills there before leaving to start his own company in 1898.

Wood did not make the mistake of imitating or copying Britains figures. He designed his own unique range of soldiers, which are, some would say, on a par with Britains. John Hill figures appear more animated and reflect the kinds of position that would be adopted by individual soldiers of the British Army in battle. The company's success derived from this animation, which contrasted sharply with Britains rigid marching or parade order toy soldiers. Johillco's products proved popular with the children of working-class families, who could identify the soldiers' poses with the military exploits of their fathers or brothers during both world

wars. Hill also issued ceremonial troops, airmen, cowboys and Indians and a vast range of other toy soldiers.

John Hill suffered two devastating blows. First, the factory was bombed during the London Blitz. The moulds somehow survived and were bought and taken to Burnley in Lancashire, where a consortium of businessmen set up a new factory, with several new issues being designed in 1955. The company had made no plans for the demise of hollow-cast figures, however, and its decision not to invest in plastic injection moulding technology dealt the company its second blow. It was forced into liquidation during the early 1960s.

Fry, Hanks and BMC had ceased trading before World War II, but of the other companies, Crescent bought out Reka in 1932 and continued to produce lead figures until 1959, and both Charbens

ABOVE
John Hill & Co. produced hollow-cast toy soldiers and figures between 1898 and 1959, and it was responsible for hundreds of items, being second only to Britains in pre-World War II production. The khaki charging figure with fixed bayonet was first made in the early 1900s, and remained in production for many years in this form, as did the charging Highlander, although this was issued in different paint versions over the years. The mounted Field Marshal with baton and the guardsman kneeling, firing are typical 1950s figures. The Highland Piper was available in many tartans and came in several grades of paint, which governed the purchase price – the more intricate the tartan, the higher the price. These figures are a mixture of sizes – 54mm (2¼in) and 90mm (3½in) high – depending on whether they are standing or kneeling.

ABOVE

"Some of the finest toy soldiers ever designed." This comment has been made of the range of US GIs made by Timpo and designed by Roy Selwyn Smith. The range, 54mm (2¼in) high, which included troops in both action and domestic poses, was available during the early 1950s. The knight was part of the King Arthur and the Knights of the Round Table set released to coincide with the MGM film. Air-gun darts were inserted into each figure's helmet to give a perfect plume.

ABOVE

Fylde Manufacturing Company produced this splendid cowboy in 1951. The hollow-cast figure is a standard 90mm (3½in) high. Fylde was taken over by John Hill & Co., which continued to produce this item.

ABOVE

Cowboys and Indians have always been popular children's toys. This Indian, produced by Harvey in the UK c.1951, is an example of the colourful, action-packed toys that were available in the years immediately following World War II. It is 54mm (2¼in) high.

ABOVE

The UK company Benbros made toy soldiers for the juvenile market during the early 1950s. The figures sold for only a few pennies and so were easily affordable. The two drummers, 54mm (2¼in) high, are part of a range of about 75 figures produced by the firm.

and Taylor & Barratt emerged in 1920. All these manufacturers were successful in making the transition to plastic production after World War II.

A handful of new companies emerged after World War II, with Timpo, short for Toy Importers, being by far the most successful. With the assistance of Roy Selwyn Smith it produced some of the best hollow-cast toy soldiers to be made in post-war years – the company was active between 1946 and 1955.

Britains toy soldiers were regarded as being for wealthier families, and they were obtainable from Harrods or from Hamleys in Regent Street, London, as well as from other up-market outlets. The figures produced by manufacturers such as Hill, Crescent and Timpo tended to be available from stores such as Woolworths or from small, independent high street shops.

On the continent and in the USA the hollow-cast method was adopted, but not to such an extent as in the UK. German

ABOVE

The coronation coach by William Britain first appeared in 1937. This example dates from 1953, when many thousands were produced, and few families in the UK would not have had some form of coronation souvenir. In its original box, this item still commands good prices at auction. It is 54mm (2¼in) high.

RIGHT

Edward Jones of Chicago made his mark on the US toy soldier market for only a short time. His soldiers, although sold through dimestores, were similar to British hollow-cast figures. This 54mm (2¼in) high Greek Evzone is, like many of Jones's pieces, rare. The Chicago Historical Society has a large display of items donated by Jones.

manufacturers, which had been the world's major suppliers of toy soldiers before 1893, preferred to stick to solid-cast items, flats or composition figures rather than turn to hollow-cast production.

French manufacturers like Mignot, LP and GM adopted hollow-casting with more enthusiasm, with Mignot producing hollow-cast versions of some of its solid soldiers, although the subject areas were mainly confined to French troops, Napoleonic regiments or action figures from World War I.

In the USA the majority of what are known as dimestore figures were made by a hollow- or slush-cast method, but Edward Jones of Chicago used more conventional hollow-casting methods, relying on the firm of Sale in Birmingham, UK to produce moulds for sale in the USA. Jones was a brilliant designer, but he was a poor businessman, and although his figures are much sought after today, he did not achieve fame during his lifetime, and in fact had a history of failed ventures and companies.

ABOVE

This French hollow-cast figure, 52mm (2⅛in) high, was manufactured by GM in Paris in the mid-1950s.

CHAPTER THREE

COMPOSITION FIGURES

Composition toy soldiers are made from a combination of materials which are used to form a figure. Papier-mâché is a kind of composition, but the most common material was achieved by mixing together sawdust, glue, kaolin and cassein, and this combination was devised in Vienna in 1898 by a company named Pfeiffer. The resulting mixture was shaped around a wire armature, left to dry and then hand-painted. The material was especially popular in Germany, and in 1926 Hausser, two brothers from Stuttgart, adopted the name Elastolin for their composition figures. This name is used today by collectors to refer to all composition figures, although strictly it should be used only for Hausser items.

ABOVE

Hausser of Germany made this 100mm (4in) guardsman at slope arms and the officer carrying a sword. Large Elastolin figures such as these formed part of the company's pre-World War II range, and they are now much sought after by collectors.

LEFT

Composition figures made in Germany before World War II nearly always depicted figures of the German armed forces. These bandsmen are typical of the multitude of figures produced in the mid-1930s. They are 65mm (2½in) in height. The oval base indicates that they are by Hausser-Elastolin rather than by Lineol, which usually used a square or oblong base.

ABOVE
The Italian company Figur Brevitt made some composition figures depicting the Vatican Guard. This piece is 60mm (2⅜in) high and was made by a process that was similar to Hausser's composition process, originally devised in Austria.

ABOVE
This composition nurse, probably made by one of the Austrian or German companies that specialized in this type of figure in the 1930s, is 65mm (2½in) high.

ABOVE
Toydell was one of only three UK manufacturers to produce plaster or composition material toy soldiers. This 100mm (4in) high Yeoman of the Guard is part of the range that was available to gift shops in Windsor during the early 1950s.

Elastolin produced 70mm (2¾in) figures from 1904 to 1943, although some of the early figures varied in size and could be as large as 100mm (4in). Most of the world's armed forces were portrayed in the Elastolin range during the 1920s, but during the 1930s the range changed to reflect the German armed forces and the rise of the Nazi regime.

Elastolin's main competition came from Lincol, which had a factory in Dresden. Lincol issued a similar range of figures to Hausser but did not actually copy the other company's products.

Both manufacturers issued figures depicting German personalities, such as Hitler, Hess and Goering, and the world record price so far paid for a single toy soldier was for a figure of Rudolf Hess. This item still commands a price of around £500 ($750). These figures were sometimes given porcelain heads, thus enhancing the facial detail.

The Italian firm of Figur Brevitt made some Elastolin-type figures, mainly depicting soldiers of the Italian army or Vatican guards, but, with the exception of Durso (Belgium) and Durolin

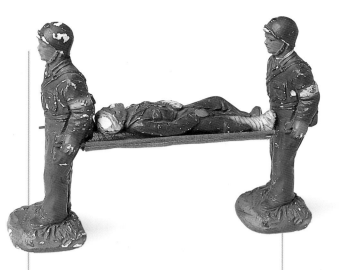

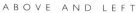

ABOVE AND LEFT

Miller plaster figures, which were available in US "five and dime" stores, depicted a field-hospital nurse and stretcher party. These 100mm (4in) plaster-of-Paris figures are prone to chipping and are collected by a minority of enthusiasts in the USA.

ABOVE

An unknown French manufacturer used composition to produce this World War I French infantryman with a standard; it is 70mm (2¾in) high.

ABOVE

Some plaster figures were produced in the UK. Although this Indian Army Sikh is more ornamental than toy-like, it was sold as a toy soldier. It is 100mm (4in) high, dates from c.1938 and is one of the few examples made from plaster.

ABOVE

Marked *Kresge* on the underside of the base, this composition British infantryman, 60mm (2⅜in) high, was sold through Kresge stores in the USA. The manufacturer is unknown, and the figure was available for only a short period after World War II.

(Czechoslovakia), few other countries outside of Germany used composition for toy soldiers.

After World War II the Brent Toy Company issued a small range of khaki infantry based on the Elastolin idea, using the name Elastolene in the UK, and Timpo introduced some small Timpolene figures to its range, but both were only stopgap measures while lead was in short supply.

Miller in the USA made some 100mm (4in) figures during the 1950s using a plaster of Paris concoction, and in the UK some large-size figures, more akin to statuettes, were issued by Riviere and Willett. All of these ventures were short-lived when the conventional lead toy soldier regained the upper hand as soon as restrictions on lead were lifted.

CHAPTER FOUR

DIMESTORE FIGURES

I n the United States toy soldiers were generally sold as
individual figures rather than in boxed sets, and they were
often found in stores such as Kresge, McCrory, Neisner, Newberry
and Woolworth. These stores were commonly known as "five and
dime stores" because they sold items costing 5 or 10 cents. In the
1930s toy soldiers, produced in a similar way to British hollow-
cast figures, were sold in these stores, and they have come to be
known as dimestore figures, although a more accurate description,
which refers to the method of manufacture, would be slush-cast
figures.

The word "dimestore" was probably first used by the collector
and researcher Don Pielin, who organizes the Chicago Old Toy
Soldier Show. Pielin and Richard O'Brien, who has written
extensively on US dimestore figures, have been responsible for
discovering much of the history and background of US-made toy
soldiers, and without their research the story of the dimestore
figure might never have achieved the recognition it deserves.

The best-known manufacturers of dimestore figures are probably
the Barclay Manufacturing Company and Manoil, both of which
began production in the 1920s. In general, Manoil and Barclay
figures are 70mm (2¾in) high, a size that is recognized as
standard for US-made toy soldiers. Grey Iron, a company that, as

ABOVE
**Soldiers carrying out domestic
duties often found their way into
dimestore ranges, and this seated
soldier with a typewriter at a
wooden table is a good example of
the genre. The figure is sometimes given the nickname
"correspondent", in reference to a
newspaper reporter. It is 75mm
(3in) high.**

RIGHT

The American Soldier Company, which used the tradename Eureka, made these figures as early as 1906. They are listed by the manufacturer as US volunteers and are 54mm (2¼in) high, a size more in keeping with UK hollow-cast toy soldiers than dimestore figures.

ABOVE

Lincoln Logs, a US company, made hollow-cast figures in the 1950s. In size and structure they more closely resemble UK-made hollow-cast figures than most US examples, and although they were sold through dimestores, they fit well with figures manufactured in the UK. The Mountie was part of a series of cowboys and Indians made by the company, while the sailor is from its standard military range. These figures are 52mm (2⅛in) high.

its name suggests, used a cast iron process, adopted the dimestore size and style for its rather solid figures, and Tommy Toy, All Nu and the Japanese-made Minikins also made standard-sized metal figures. However, McLoughlin, Jones, Lincoln Logs and Warren, other notable US makers, made toy soldiers more in keeping with the UK size of 54mm (2¼in). Other soldiers retailed through dimestores and now keenly collected in the US include the rubber figures made by Auburn and the plaster ones made by Miller.

BARCLAY MANUFACTURING COMPANY

Barclay, which was founded in 1924 by partners and brothers Donze and Michael Levy, operated in West Hoboken, New Jersey, and it grew from humble beginnings to become the largest manufacturer of toy soldiers and figures in the USA, with the factory later moving to Union City and West New York.

The nucleus of the company's production was, not surprisingly, devoted to portraying models of US armed forces, mostly in action, and cowboys, Indians and other figures depicting the old Wild West. The khaki troops made before 1939 had removable tin helmets, although post-war figures had fixed helmets. After 1945 the figures' bases were removed and the feet on each soldier were widened so that it was free-standing without the need of a base. This system was responsible for the advent of the nickname "pod-foot" to describe figures made by this method. The purpose of the method was to conserve lead which had become more expensive by the removal of the base.

ABOVE

This Manoil dimestore anti-aircraft gun and gunner is 75mm (3in) high. The legs of the Barclay version are together, which would have made casting this intricate figure easier.

ABOVE

Barclay's kneeling nurse is similar in design to the Elastolin and composition nurses made in Germany. It is 75mm (3in) high.

ABOVE

This naval ensign from Manoil's range demonstrates the similarities between Barclay and Manoil figures. Even though the companies' dimestore figures were not direct copies, there were, in fact, only a limited number of possible poses in which the soldiers could be produced, given the manufacturing processes involved. This figure is 75mm (3in) in height.

ABOVE

Grey Iron made this seated machine gunner in the 1930s when the company made a range of dimestore figures. It is 75mm (3in) high.

ABOVE

Barclay made this dimestore pod-foot soldier kneeling, firing in the 1950s. The red uniform is scarce, and the figure is thought to have been made to represent enemy troops from the Korean War. It is 75mm (3in) high.

Barclay deviated from the 70mm (2¾in) standard size figure only rarely, although some 45mm (1¾in) items were made which were mainly scaled-down versions of dimestore figures. The company's output included pirates, knights, sailors, Japanese troops, motorcycle and sidecar combinations, parachutists and firemen, as well as ranges of civilian items depicting the social history of the USA both before and after World War II.

Barclay continued to supply dimestores after World War II, when similar changes in taste took place on both sides of the Atlantic; plastic was being developed and dimestore production was phased out towards the end of the 1950s. Barclay ceased trading in 1971, having scaled down its production since 1965. Plastic soldiers had monopolized the market and the demand for lead had faded. There is no indication that Barclay ever contemplated plastic production.

ABOVE
Listed in the Manoil catalogue as M88 parachute jumper, this is another example of the variety of poses used by the makers of dimestore figures. Many other examples in the company's ranges reveal this animation and the skilful design techniques. It is 75mm (3in) high.

BELOW
Barclay dimestore World War II grenade thrower, 1935. It is 75mm (3in) in height.

MANOIL

Maurice and Jack Manoil joined with Walter Baetz in 1924 to found the company that bears their name. It produced soldiers that were similar in scale and style to those made by Barclay, but unlike the UK, no actual imitation took place. Although Manoil's figures tended to cover the same areas as Barclay, each item was different, perhaps with just an ounce more character than Barclay. The Manoil Happy Farm civilian range was produced to reflect US social history and, like Barclay, the company produced a wide range of military vehicles.

OTHER US MANUFACTURERS

Grey Iron used the same dimestore scale as Manoil and Barclay, but its figures were produced in cast iron. They seem to suffer more from paint loss than Barclay and Manoil.

Home-cast toy soldiers were very popular in the US in the 1930s. Casting sets containing metal moulds, a bar of lead, a ladle

LEFT
This soldier operating a searchlight was cast as one piece by Barclay. It proved to be a popular figure and was issued as many as seven times, each time with minor details added to or deleted from the casting. It is 75mm (3in) high.

RIGHT
The threat of gas attacks provided manufacturers with an alternative subject for their figures. Playwood Plastics made this composition soldier, which wears a gas mask and holds a flare gun. It is 75mm (3in) high.

RIGHT
This curious dimestore flat figure made in 1952 has a rather comic appearance. The reason for its issue is unclear, but it may have been meant as a novelty item to be placed around the base of a Christmas tree. It is 70mm (2¾in) high.

and a melting-pot for the boy to make his own soldiers at home became popular, in particular with children in remote areas of the USA where no department stores were evident. They were available through mail order. Sachs was perhaps the best-known manufacturer along with Henry Schiercke. The soldiers were mainly US figures.

Macys department store in central New York sold home-cast moulds and dimestore figures although it also imported goods from Britains, John Hill, Crescent, Cherilea, Barrett and Sons and F.G. Taylor and Sons from the UK.

In the mid-1980s Ron Eccles of Burlington, Iowa, who had acquired many of Barclay's and Manoil's original moulds, began to cast and produce excellent copies of the famous dimestore soldiers. Ron's wife, Debbie, produces a catalogue of their products and paints the items in a style that evokes the charm and character of the original toys. Each item is marked *Eccles Brothers* with the current date, and is issued as a reproduction of the original soldiers.

OCCUPIED JAPAN

Japanese-made toy soldiers were also sold through the "five and dime stores" and can, therefore, be classed as dimestore figures. After World War II many US companies imported lead, composition and celluloid toy soldiers from Japan, many of which were copies of US or European products. The quality of the items was variable – Minikins, for example, were made of lead and were of high quality, while Trico made crude composition figures. Nevertheless, all were sold in vast numbers and have a strong following among today's collectors, with items in boxes marked *Occupied Japan* being of particular value. Minikins were also exported to the UK and to France, where many were purchased by the US GIs as gifts for their children in the USA.

RIGHT
The manufacturer of this solid, 54mm (2¼in) high West Point Cadet is not known, but the figure was made in occupied Japan just after World War II and was probably destined for sale as a souvenir item in the West Point Academy area. It was also available through US "five and dime" stores.

ABOVE
The unusual Indian, 54mm (2¼in) high, marked *Made in Japan*, could be a product of US-occupied Japan, but it looks as if it was made during the 1930s. It has a pivot through the body so that both arms can move, which is a very unusual feature in a toy soldier.

CHAPTER FIVE

PLASTIC FIGURES

ABOVE

Beton of the USA was one of the earliest companies to produce plastic figures. There were self-coloured, 60mm (2⅜in) high, and the range was limited to US infantry soldiers, which were sold through dimestores in the US and Woolworths in the UK. They were probably the first examples of plastic toy soldiers to be available after World War II.

Although experiments into using plastic as a commercial material for toy soldiers took place in the mid-1930s, it was not until the late 1940s that a viable product was produced. It is uncertain which manufacturer can lay claim to the first plastic toy soldiers. In the US Beton was certainly supplying dimestores with unpainted 60mm (2⅜in) figures of US battledress troops just after World War II, while in England hard, brittle plastic soldiers and cowboys and Indians were offered for sale by Airfix in 1947. Malleable Mouldings of Deal, Kent, imported from F. Winkler through Eire a range of hard plastic figures, designed by Holger Eriksson, and although the design was superior to anything produced before 1947, the venture failed, probably because the figures were sophisticated and collectors of lead toy soldiers were reluctant to change materials.

Plastic figures are made by the process of injection moulding, in which the raw material is forced through holes in the centre of a brass mould by a power-assisted injection machine. Some of the companies that had issued hollow-cast figures had their moulds converted to fit the plastic injection moulding machines by removing the wooden handles from the hollow moulds and altering the lead escape holes. Timpo, Cherilea and Crescent which all began to produce plastic figures around 1955 adopted this

Malleable Mouldings pioneered the commercial production of plastic figures in the late 1940s in the UK. These two examples – a mounted Roundhead and a guardsman at the slope – are rare because the venture was not a commercial success, perhaps being a little before its time. They are 54mm (2¼in) and 90mm (3½in) high respectively.

procedure before designing new moulds. The first UK maker to issue plastic figures, Zang Products (later Herald), operated in East London. Zang employed a number of designers during the early 1950s, and the factory produced some of the finest plastic toy soldiers ever made. Khaki battledress infantry, American Civil War soldiers, Foot Guards, Life Guards, Horse Guards, Highlanders, cowboys and Indians, Trojan warriors and an Indian Army Sikh appeared during the early 1950s, packed in attractive, colourful boxes or on display cards of four figures, which quickly became popular with children. In 1953 the tradename Herald was adopted and a logo of a medieval herald inspired by the trademark used at the Harrogate toy trade fair was embossed on the underside of each figure's base.

John Hill & Co. of Burnley, Britains' main competitors, converted some of its hollow-cast moulds to plastic in the early 1950s, but although their employees urged the company to invest in injection moulding equipment it was reluctant to change, believing that plastic would be a short-lived phase. The firm of Kelloggs approached Hill to supply hundreds of thousands of figures to be put in cornflake packages. Hill was not convinced and lost the contract to its rival, Crescent. This was the beginning of the end for John Hill & Co., which ceased trading in the late 1950s.

This plastic King Arthur by Timpo has a good quality paint finish. It was part of a series issued in the mid-1960s, and the unpainted figure was also available in boxes entitled "Action Pack" which contained around 20 other figures. It is 54mm (2¼in) high.

Herald Trojan Warriors, 54mm (2¼in) high, were introduced by M. Zang in the 1950s, and continued to be produced by Britains, later in Hong Kong. Also included in this set was a mounted general with a standard on a white horse.

ABOVE AND LEFT

The Herald figures issued by M. Zang in the early 1950s must, in the following 30 years or so, have been produced by the million. The ten examples shown, 45mm (1¾in), 54mm (2¼in) and 90mm (3½in) respectively, are some of the most often seen plastic toy soldiers, and they are from larger sets. The cowboys and Indians series also included mounted figures; the Highlanders had a mounted officer; and the British Army khaki troops were printed in grey and issued as enemy troops. Household Cavalry troops were joined by foot guards and were sold not only in toy shops but in souvenir and gift shops in London. When Britains took over the Herald range, it retained and added to these sets. Production was moved to Hong Kong, but this resulted in a decline in the quality of the castings. Nevertheless, they remained popular and graced toy-shop shelves for many years until the disappearance of the Herald range in the late 1970s.

ABOVE

Turkey is an unlikely country to have produced plastic toy soldiers. This set of Turkish warriors, each 60mm (2⅜in) high, was purchased in the late 1970s in one of the many bazaars in Istanbul.

ABOVE

AHI of Hong Kong made this hollow-cast American Civil War infantryman, 54mm (2¼in) in height. This figure is unusual in that it is a copy of Herald plastic soldiers, made in 1955 in an attempt by this Hong Kong manufacturer to revive the hollow-cast process.

BRITAINS LTD

Around 1953 Britains Ltd, which had been watching the success of Herald's plastic figures, formed an association with Herald Miniatures, which eventually resulted in Britains taking over the Herald name and company. Britains continued to issue the bulk of its plastic soldiers under the Herald name, which remained part of the Britains tradename for its plastic figures until the late 1970s or early 1980s. In 1959 Britains started to introduce other ranges of plastics as its hollow-cast lead production scaled down. About this time an ironic reversal in toy soldier production occurred – in 1957 lead copies of the plastic Herald figures began to be imported from Hong Kong to the USA and UK. It was as though lead toy soldiers were making a final attempt to regain popularity, although legislation in the UK prohibiting lead in toys eventually ended this practice.

Just as Britains had revolutionized the toy soldier industry with the introduction of hollow-cast figures, its introduction of Swoppets revolutionized the world of plastic figures. The Swoppet range included foot and mounted cowboys, Indians and knights with interchangeable heads, bodies and legs, and even individual weapons. In 1960 the company introduced another new range when it reverted to the ceremonial or full-dress type of toy soldier, but with some Swoppet-type features. The range was called Eyes Right, and, as the name suggests, the heads were movable as were the arms. The range began with guardsmen, Royal Marines and other regiments, and it was later extended to include US Marine

Britains made this plastic Swoppet cowboy, 54mm (2¼in) high, seated on a barrel. All the pieces, including individual pistols, are removable and so could be "swopped" with other figures in the range.

and US and UK Army bands. The final Eyes Right figures, the officers and men of the Bahamas Police and foot and mounted Royal Canadian Mounted Police, appeared in 1962.

The Swoppet range was extended in 1962 by the introduction of battledress infantry. American Civil War foot figures had formed part of the Herald range from the early 1950s, but it took some 10 years for the mounted troops of a Swoppet variety to join them. The old foot figures were phased out and replaced by a newly designed set. Most of the existing ranges were extended, with siege weapons being added in 1967 to enhance the Swoppet range of knights.

Deetail figures, which were plastic with a lead base, first appeared in 1971. The range initially consisted of US and German World War II infantrymen. Herald plastic production had been sub-contracted to a Hong Kong company in 1972 because it was cheaper to have the range manufactured in Hong Kong and shipped to the UK than it was to produce the figures in the UK. It

ABOVE AND LEFT
The Britains Eyes Right range was an attempt to reintroduce ceremonial-style British soldiers to the toy market and to fill, in part, the gap left by the discontinued hollow-cast range. The figures, at 54mm (2¼in) high, have movable heads and arms. The piper is a Scots Guard, and there is a paper banner on the bagpipes. The Royal Canadian Mounted Policeman was later issued on a lead base in the Deetail range. The Scots Guards and Royal Marines were joined by bands marching and at attention. Britains kept pace with military changes by issuing the soldiers with the new-style rifle as it appeared and by replacing the slope arms version.

RIGHT

Although they were not an official part of the Britains Eyes Right range, American Civil War and War of Independence figures were issued with movable heads and arms. In part, the American Civil War Union and Confederate figures were issued to replace the long-standing Herald versions, and there was a transitional period in which the fixed-limb Herald figures were phased out and the first of the movable-limb infantry figures were introduced. Examples of both ranges, 54mm (2¼in) and 90mm (3½in) high respectively, are shown here. The standard bearers have paper flags.

ABOVE

These American War of Independence figures, 54mm (2¼in) high, were made by Britains. National guns of the period are also shown. The series was reintroduced in 1976 to coincide with the American Bicentennial celebrations.

is interesting to note that in the Deetail range lead was again featuring in the production of toy soldiers. From its initially limited range, Deetail figures expanded to include Japanese soldiers, 8th Army personnel, members of the Afrika Korps, Apaches, Foreign Legionnaires, Arab and Mexican warriors, paratroopers, infantrymen in battledress, US Civil War and Napoleonic troops. Turks and Medieval knights were added, and several series of spacemen were issued during the 1980s. As New Metal Models have taken on an increasingly important role in the Britains range, the range of plastic figures has diminished, the most recent range being the Knights of the Sword figures.

OTHER UK MANUFACTURERS

A multitude of manufacturers, small and large, established and new, thrived between 1955 and 1979. All have much to offer the toy soldier enthusiast.

Timpo, whose lead figures had been of exceptional quality, relied at first on converting existing moulds, which it did with a

ABOVE AND LEFT

ABOVE AND LEFT
Britains Deetail figures appeared in the toy shops in the 1970s, at 54mm (2¼in) high. These fixed-limb, plastic figures stood on metal bases, and many ranges were introduced, aimed at children rather than at adult collectors. The range included a landrover and gun; US infantrymen, complete with recoil rifles; British khaki-clad infantry with camouflage helmets; and the 8th Army with Vickers machine gun. Japanese and German infantry were enhanced by the introduction of vehicles to accompany each series, and French Foreign Legion and Arab figures were joined by historical subjects, including English, French and Scottish troops at the Napoleonic wars and Turks in combat with medieval knights. Although it is barely 20 years since the first Deetail figures were issued, there is already a growing band of adult collectors avidly trying to acquire full sets of figures that they may first have owned in childhood. The range also included cowboys and Indians, including Apaches, and the 7th Cavalry, but these have not yet become as desirable as the other Deetail sets.

ABOVE
Britains' Deetail Napoleonic troops, both foot soldiers and mounted, 54mm (2¼in) and 90mm (3½in) high respectively.

ABOVE
Knights of the Helm was an attempt by Timpo to incorporate more detail into its Swoppet-style range of plastic figures. This knight has an ornate head-dress, for example, and the series is keenly sought after by collectors of plastic figures. It is 54mm (2¼in) high.

degree of success. It produced King Arthur and the Knights of the Round Table, which could also be purchased unpainted in boxes marked *Action Pack*. Timpo adopted a Swoppet-type system in a large way, and this move enabled the company to survive for longer than many of its competitors. It increased production to gigantic proportions, introducing hundreds of different toy soldiers by means of the interchangeable method. Knights and Roman soldiers complete with chariots, khaki-clad troops, paratroopers and World War II Germans, cowboys and Indians, and Mexicans were all part of the range, distributed from the factory in Shotts, Lanarkshire. Norman Tooth, who had worked for Timpo from the late 1940s and had designed many Timpo items, continued to come up with new ideas to bolster the ailing toy soldier industry throughout the mid-1970s. Set pieces, consisting of figures and accessories, included cowboys branding cattle, Indians sending smoke signals from a fire, and searchlight, machine gun and artillery units to enhance the modern battledress troops. Mr Tooth devised a remarkable machine that would convert, cut, paint and assemble a complete figure. This automatic process produced Timpo's last range in 1978 – a series of Vikings, on foot and mounted – and Timpo ceased production in 1979.

Initially, Timpo lost ground to Cherilea, Crescent, Lone Star and Charbens, which had seized the opportunity to enter the arena with plastic toy soldiers. Cherilea, whose figures were 60mm (2⅜in) high, introduced many new ranges, including soldiers in battledress and paratroopers, Chinese and German soldiers, and 8th Army troops, complete with a figure of Field Marshal Montgomery. A rival series was brought out by Timpo. Cherilea

LEFT
This plastic mounted Viking was one of the last pieces to be made by Timpo by means of the revolutionary new machinery designed by R.N. Tooth. The Viking, which has a movable head and waist, is 90mm (3½in) high.

LEFT
This plastic Mexican bandit with a money pouch was part of an animated Wild West set made by Crescent. The set was one of several produced by Crescent in 60mm (2⅜in) scale.

LEFT
Cherilea made this unusual Chinese infantryman with a flame-thrower in the 1960s. Only a few examples of this 60mm (2⅜in) piece were made, and the series of six is rare.

issued historical sets, including Roundheads, Cavaliers, medieval knights and a Tudor execution set. Lone Star made ceremonial troops, German Afrika Korps and naval figures in action, as well as the obligatory cowboys and Indians, and Charbens repeated much of these subject areas but also produced pirates, Cossacks and a bull-fighting set. Crescent introduced a superb series of British World War I troops, and also produced knights, Robin Hood, cowboys and Indians and guardsmen, which were eventually obtainable in cereal packets.

Smaller companies, such as Trojan, Speedwell, VP, UNA, Benbros, Gemodels, Kentoys and Sacul, survived for a short while, and by the late 1970s only Cavendish Miniatures of Windsor, still in production, Airfix, whose unpainted soldiers have sold by the million, Timpo and Britains remained. Cavendish Miniatures also specializes in souvenir items made of solid lead

ABOVE
This plastic mounted cowboy, in a fringed, Cheyenne-type jacket, has a movable head and waist and is one of a large series of such figures produced by Timpo in its range of Swoppet-style figures in the 1970s. It stands 54mm (2¼in) high.

This plastic World War I grenade thrower, 56mm (2¼in) high, was part of a series of nine figures manufactured by Crescent in the 1960s. This subject was largely ignored by manufacturers of plastic figures, which makes this item, and the other five foot, and three mounted, soldiers in the series, quite scarce.

Poplar Playthings, a company from Wales, made this Roman chariot and charioteer, 80mm (3⅛in) high. Although the figures are classed as plastic by collectors, they are actually made of rubber. The company enjoyed minor success with its toy figures in the mid-1950s. It is thought that it may have sold its moulds to a US manufacturer.

The UK company Dorset Soldiers purchased the Cherilea moulds in the late 1980s and reissued many of the former company's lines during the early 1990s. This Tudor-style swordsman was one of these figures; it was produced in self-coloured plastic and stands 60mm (2⅜in) high.

but have also been supplying the trade with plastic figures on a wholesale basis for at least 25 years. At one stage they bought up the remaining stocks of Britains Eyes Right figures. By the end of the 1970s, with the exception of the Cavendish range and cheap imports from Hong Kong, Britains had the field almost to itself.

A new aspect of plastic toy soldier production emerged in 1989, when Giles Brown of Dorset Soldiers purchased many of the former Cherilea plastic moulds and started to issue the unpainted figures in self-coloured plastic. These figures were at a price just right for the collector who could not afford the original Cherilea items, which were becoming sought-after by collectors. Marlborough of Wales bought the redundant Charbens moulds in 1990 and started a similar business in the reissue of Charbens items. Toyway now holds the Timpo tradename and is issuing the former Timpo range.

ABOVE

This large 150mm (6in) high figure of a US World War II infantryman was made by Marx. These unpainted figures, which were made in Germany, Wales, Hong Kong and the USA, were sold through Woolworths stores during the 1960s.

ABOVE

Louis Marx dominated toy soldier production in the USA. This Robin Hood, which is 60mm (2⅜in) high, was popular in the 1960s. The figures were available painted or unpainted in self-coloured plastic, and the name of each character was embossed in the base.

ABOVE

Few holiday-makers to Greece can have failed to notice the striking uniform of the Evzone. Aeoha of Greece produces this plastic figure as part of a series that is available at most tourist attractions in Athens. They are 65mm (2½in) high.

US PLASTIC FIGURES

In the United States plastic toy soldiers were available from a number of companies – Beton's early efforts were followed by small ranges from Lido and Ausley – but the market was dominated by Louis Marx & Co. This famous and well-respected toy company was best known for its tinplate toys, and it specialized in the production of large boxed display sets, known as playsets, which included not only toy soldiers but buildings and accessories to enable the child to gain additional play value from the toys. Sets sometimes included over 100 figures, and although they were unpainted, they dominated the US market for 30 years.

Painted Marx soldiers were available in the Warriors of the World series. Almost all periods of history as well as the world's major conflicts were covered by Marx at one time or another. The company also issued 150mm (6in) high figures, and both hard and soft plastics were used for all ranges. Marx opened factories in Germany, Hong Kong and Swansea in Wales.

Marx issued up to 100 self-coloured plastic figures in sets, which were supplied to collectors in the 1960s through Sears Roebuck, the US chain of department stores. The examples shown, 60mm (2⅜in) high, are modern reproductions by Michael Ellis of Marksmen, who acquired the rights to issue some of the original Marx range.

Benbros, VP, UNA and many Hong Kong manufacturers produced copies of Herald pieces, especially the khaki-clad infantry series. This example by VP can hardly be distinguished from the Herald version. Indeed, some collectors specialize in obtaining as many different examples of these figures as possible. This figure is 54mm (2¼in) in height.

Marx has become a cult with collectors, and items are avidly collected. So popular have they become that a collectors' magazine specifically covering playsets is issued in the USA.

The idea of using and reissuing Marx figures was seized upon by Michael Ellis of Acton, London, and his company, Marksmen, is carving out a lucrative slice of the modern toy soldier market.

······ EUROPEAN PLASTIC FIGURES ······

Apart from the many Hong Kong companies, who almost without exception resorted to copying or pirating US and European designs, the continent of Europe was the main source of plastic figures, with Australasia, Scandinavia and South America playing no part in toy soldier production.

Companies in France, Germany, Italy, Spain and the former USSR have produced various quantities, and a diverse quality, of plastic toy soldiers. Starlux of France used hard plastic to depict a wide range of French Napoleonic troops, Foreign Legionnaires and military school cadets. The figures were realistically modelled in good action poses with a high level of detail on the paint finish, and towards the peak of production Starlux issued all manner of subjects, including the more unusual Wild West, backwoodsmen, pirates, medieval knights, Romans and Gauls. It also issued a second grade series of toy soldiers, slightly smaller than 54mm (2¼in), which was aimed at the lower end of the market. Starlux exhibited at the Earls Court Toy Fair in 1991, but at the time of writing reports suggest that production has ceased. Other small companies existed in France, with Jean, for example, issuing items with the minimum detail and finish.

In Germany Elastolin, which had been famous before World War II for its composition figures, was keen to supply the toy

BELOW
When it stopped using the composition process, Elastolin, Hausser used plastic, and this 100mm (4in) mounted German officer, which can be taken from the horse, is plastic. The pre-war Nazi influence is still evident in this piece, whose design is similar to the pre-war composition soldiers produced by Hausser before the factory was bombed.

ABOVE
After World War II Hausser abandoned composition and turned to plastic. This Royal Canadian Mounted Policeman would have been aimed at the souvenir market in Canada. It is 65mm (2½in) high and was purchased in Edinburgh during the 1960s, while the Mounties were appearing at the Military Tattoo in that city.

ABOVE
Plastic toy soldiers made in Hong Kong flooded the world market for many years. These were usually unpainted and sometimes well-detailed, but they are always classed as second grade. This US infantryman in grey plastic, which is 80mm (3⅛in) high, is typical of this range.

ABOVE
This plastic copy of a Swoppet-style cowboy with a movable waist and head was made in Hong Kong and is 52mm (2⅛in) high.

soldier market again. Unfortunately, the occupying Allied nations imposed restrictions on the production of "war-like" toys, a constraint that was only slowly relaxed. Elastolin favoured hard plastic substances and returned to production with a series of large-scale Romans, knights and cowboys and Indians, which were based on some of its pre-war designs. Later it made some German World War II troops, and its range was issued until the late 1970s, when it too fell victim to the new technology-style toys now popular with children. Gaugemaster of the UK has recently tried to revive the plastic Elastolin range, but with limited success.

Spain's main producer of toy soldiers was Reamsa, whose range included many figures from the Spanish armed forces as well as medieval characters, Moors of the Riff (Spanish Colonial troops) and other figures from Spanish history. Popular from the 1950s

A rare plastic figure, 52mm (2⅛in) high, made in France by Quiralux, of a toytown soldier at port arms. The moulds for this series were sold during the early 1950s to Wend-Al in the UK, which converted them for use with aluminium and sold the figures produced from them, which were described as "unbreakable", with great success throughout the 1950s.

ABOVE

Reamsa of Spain made plastic figures during the 1960s, concentrating on figures of the Spanish armed forces. This 60mm (2⅜in) high Spanish Army standard bearer is one of a set of 20 pieces.

ABOVE

Starlux of France is the dominant force in the production of plastic figures in continental Europe, and it has only recently scaled down its issues to the UK. The medieval court jester is from its first-grade range; the paratrooper, on the other hand, is a second-grade figure of slightly smaller proportions, which sold for less than the more detailed and intricately painted items. The female Russian soldier is a departure from the company's normal output, very few manufacturers having released female toy soldiers. These figures are 54mm (2¼in) high.

until the 1970s, Reamsa toy soldiers are now being reissued by an enterprising collector, Ric Bracamontes, of Company B, which operates from the Chicago area in the USA. Reamsa itself ceased trading in the late 1970s.

In Italy the toy soldier market has been and, at the time of writing, still is dominated by Atlantic, which began production in the early 1970s. The company has adapted its production methods and style to the Marx concept, preferring to issue boxed sets of unpainted figures representing the Italian armed forces. Early sets included a series of major world military leaders and their armed forces. Unpainted figures of Mussolini, Hitler, Lenin and Mao featured in some sets. Comansi, another Italian company, issue many unpainted sets of Wild West items, as does Nardi, which includes US Civil War troops with movable waists.

CHAPTER SIX

NEW TOY SOLDIERS

ABOVE

One of the earliest manufacturers of New Toy Soldiers was Mark Time of Croydon, London, which produced figures during the mid-1970s. The volunteer cyclist is an unusual item from the range. It is 54mm (2¼in) high.

When the production of hollow-cast toy soldiers came to an end in 1966, plastic toy soldiers, solid military miniature items and discontinued hollow-cast figures were the only choices open to the toy soldier collector. However, the situation changed in 1973, when New Toy Soldiers burst onto the market, almost simultaneously from two non-related sources.

U K PRODUCTION

Frank and Jan Scroby were perhaps the first to recognize that there was a demand for toy soldiers made in the style of the no-longer-made hollow-cast figures. The Scrobys had been selling old hollow-cast figures from their stall on Portobello Road Market, London, but these were becoming difficult to obtain. They experimented with non-toxic, white metal substances and developed their own range of what are now known as New Toy Soldiers. This all-embracing title is applied to all solid, white metal toy soldiers and figures designed, manufactured and painted in the style of, and complimentary to, the old-style hollow-cast figures. Indeed, this was the original intention of the Scrobys – that is, to produce new items that would fit into a collection of existing hollow-cast figures that were no longer available.

Blenheim, the name of the street in which the Scrobys were living, was the name chosen to launch the range, which was an

ABOVE AND RIGHT
The Blenheim Highlander at the slope "steps" off on the opposite foot to most toy soldiers. The Zulu and his enemy are animated pieces and something of a departure from the standard marching figures, which were Blenheim's trademark. All stand 54mm (2¼in) high.

ABOVE
Makers of New Toy Soldiers often accept special commissions. This soldier from the Boxer Rebellion was made by Blenheim for a well-known collector in the 1970s. It is 54mm (2¼in) high.

ABOVE
Manufacturers of New Toy Soldiers were always looking for new ideas to enhance their range. This Chelsea Pensioner by Blenheim fits in with military figures, and it can be used in scenes where spectators are viewing a parade. It is 54mm (2¼in) high.

instant success with a collecting fraternity that had been starved of a traditional toy soldier for some seven years. For the purist, the Blenheim range raised a small problem in that the toy soldiers stepped off on the "wrong" foot. But this was a minor irritation, quickly overlooked by collectors anxious to purchase these miniature masterpieces.

Shamus Wade, a long-established leader in the sale of old toy soldiers, was equally quick to recognize the potential of this new venture. He entered into an agreement with the Scrobys to produce for him an exclusive range, named Nostalgia, which would be sold by him through his regular mail order lists. The sets and individual figures were produced in limited numbers and were to depict units of regiments of the British Commonwealth. The subject matter, although sometimes obscure, brought forth a unique range of New Toy Soldier regiments. During its latter years the Nostalgia range was taken over by Peter Cowan and Andrew Rose as the Blenheim range became more successful. At the time Frank and Jan Scroby were starting their private venture in London, Britains Ltd seem to have woken up to the fact that a tremendous void had been left by the disappearance of hollow-cast lead figures. The company issued a die-cast lead marching Guardsman on a thick green die-cast

LEFT

Trophy made these New Toy Soldiers depicting officers of the West India Regiment, the Indian Army and the Royal Marines. These earlier issues from Trophy were produced to fill the gap left by the ending of hollow-cast manufacture and are all 54mm (2¼in) high.

LEFT

This solid Bethnal Green volunteer, 54mm (2¼in) high, was manufactured during the mid-1970s by John Tunstill as part of his Soldiers Soldiers range. Tunstill, whose shop, Soldiers, was in Lambeth, London, made this figure to be sold exclusively as a souvenir by the Bethnal Green Museum of Childhood in London.

base of the kind used for the plastic Deetail range. The soldier's busby was plastic and the overall size was somewhat larger than the previous standard hollow-cast range, but it was a step in the right direction and the start of yet another toy soldier revolution.

As in the early days of hollow-cast figures, the Scrobys' successful venture resulted in the emergence of many other New Toy Soldier manufacturers. However, rather than imitating the Blenheim figures, the new manufacturers produced their own individual ranges. It was as if the idea had been lying dormant in their minds, needing only the stimulus supplied by the Scrobys to make the first move. Andrew Rose, a talented designer, has played a part in designing ranges for several companies, including his own range of Bastion and Wessex figures, which are still available at the time of writing.

In the mid- to late 1970s many manufacturers came and went – Gunner, Mark Time, British Bulldog, Albion, B.G. of G.B., Trafalgar, Militia, Jacklex, Empire, Campaign and M.J. Mode, for example. Some have been revived or have merged under new ownership; others have taken their place.

John Tunstill, who had retail premises in Lambeth, London, devised his own range entitled Soldiers Soldiers, which was partly

LEFT

Trophy of Wales produces a wide range of solid New Toy Soldiers. This Lancer officer was one of the company's earliest efforts – it was

made c.1974. The figure's oval base was discontinued soon afterwards, thus helping to identify the figure as an early issue. It is the standard size – 54mm (2¼in) high.

RIGHT

"Young Winston", Sir Winston Churchill, mounted and firing a pistol at an attacking Dervisher 54mm (2¼in) high, is one of a large range of New Toy Soldiers, 90mm (3½in) high, made by the Welsh company, Trophy Miniatures. The range includes a superb series of Rorke's Drift figures from the Zulu War.

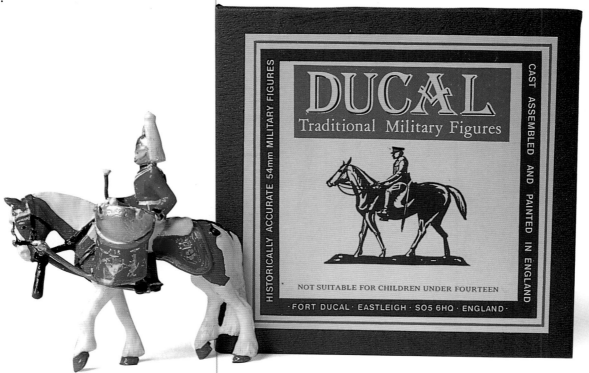

ABOVE

Thelma and Jack Duke of Ducal produce a wide selection of ceremonial troops depicting many state occasions, but they specialize in making figures to recreate Trooping the Colour. The 90mm (3½in) high Household Cavalry drum horse with its attractive box is typical of the high quality of New Toy Soldiers produced by this firm.

designed by Andrew Rose. The first issues appeared in 1977, and although the range is no longer in production, items from Soldiers Soldiers are still available through existing stocks.

Gerrard Haley of West Yorkshire started his own range, entitled Quality Model Soldiers. During the late 1970s Gerrard of Northern Toy Soldiers, a well-respected dealer in old lead figures, commenced production of his own range of New Toy Soldiers based on the armies of the Franco-Prussian war. The list of former and current manufacturers of New Toy Soldiers in the UK is almost

ABOVE

Hitler and other Nazi leaders and troops are often portrayed by New Toy Soldier companies, eager to supply the demand from collectors for figures from this period. Charles Hall of Edinburgh produced this 70mm (2¾in) high example.

ABOVE AND LEFT

These are examples of the packaging used by Frank and Jan Scroby when they were producing Blenheim and Marlborough Models. Blenheim blue boxes had gold inserts with slots for each figure. The Marlborough boxes had foam inserts and sections in which each 54mm (2¼in) high figure lay.

RIGHT

Martin Tabony sculptured, painted, designed and produced this 54mm (2¼in) high group, which is entitled "The Home Coming". Martin is one of a growing band of toy soldier manufacturers in the UK to operate as a cottage industry.

ABOVE

Andrew Rose, a talented designer, was responsible for these two 54mm (2½in) high figures in tropical service dress, which were issued under the Bastion range. Rose has designed for many New Toy Soldier manufacturers since he was associated with the Nostalgia range.

endless. Of the major companies, Trophy of Wales, which is run by Len Taylor, has become world famous for quality of design and painting. The Zulu War features heavily in the Trophy range, and new designs and historical periods of military history are constantly available from the main office in Wales or through its agents MKL, of the Guards Toy Soldier Centre, Wellington Barracks, London.

Ducal of Hampshire specializes in figures to recreate ceremonial occasions, such as the Trooping the Colour, and it will supply through its superb range enough toy soldiers to recreate any major procession.

The Blenheim range ceased in 1982 after financial difficulties, but the Scrobys introduced a new range, Marlborough, later that year, which was at first to be sold through a US agent, Star Collectables. A magnificent series in the form of the Delhi Durbar of 1902, was later introduced. This series was devised so that the collector could add to the set over a period and ultimately build a complete Durbar. Sadly, as I write Marlborough has fallen victim to the economic recession and has ceased trading.

Dorset Soldiers, owned by Giles Brown in Wiltshire, started in 1979, and it has gone from strength to strength. A wide range of UK and foreign regiments can be obtained, and new additions notified by means of a loose-leaf colour catalogue are regularly announced.

The list of UK manufacturers of New Toy Soldiers is almost endless, as can be seen from the following list of participants in the 1993 British Toy Soldier and Figure Show, Europe's largest toy

ABOVE
These Steadfast New Toy Soldiers, 54mm (2¼in) high, depict the Black Watch complete with maxim gun and officer. They form an attractive set, which is enhanced by the box.

soldier event. Many of these participants are private individuals, who manufacture for pleasure, others may be regarded as cottage industries of varying size, while those already mentioned in the text are full-time professional manufacturers: All The Queens Men, Bob Andrews, Autocraft, Ian Butcher, Carnegie Miniatures, R.P. Dew, Dorset, Ducal, Ensign, Errol John Studios, T. Felton, Frontline, Fusilier, Glebe, Great Britain and the Empire, G.M. Toy Soldiers, Good Soldiers, Highlander Miniatures, H.M. of G.B., Imperial, J.G. Miniatures, Langley Miniatures, Little Legion, Moorvale Models, Moulded Oldies, Mulberry Miniatures, Music in Miniature, R. Newth-Gibbs, Old Hall Miniatures, Onslow Militaire, Perrott – London Gauntlet, Phina, Red Box Toy Soldier Company, Replica Models, Rosedale, Sarum Soldiers, Small Potentials, Steadfast, M. Tabony, Toy Army Workshops, Tommy Atkins, Tradition, Trophy, Under the Greenwood, Unicorn and Whittlesey Miniatures. In addition, Garbaldi of Italy, Dietz and Bill Hocker from the USA, and Georg Biettron of France provided New Toy Soldiers from overseas.

ABOVE
This New Toy Soldier, representing the Royal Military Police, was made by Major Gavin Thompson, himself a member of the RMP. It is 54mm (2¼in) high. Major Thompson is a hobbyist who manufactures under the name of Kidogo.

Two retired army officers presenting each other with boxes of toy soldiers form an unusual group, made by two New Toy Soldier manufacturers on opposite sides of the world. Luigi Toiati of Garibaldi in Italy and Bill Hocker of California produced these 54mm (2¼in) high figures and gave them to the author.

ABOVE

This Highland Piper of the '45, 54mm (2¼in) high, was made by Luigi Toiati, Italy's foremost maker of New Toy Soldiers, under the tradename Garibaldi.

RIGHT

Bill Hocker of Berkeley, California, is one of the world's leading manufacturers of New Toy Soldiers. This set of a naval band is shrink-wrapped so that collectors can display the set without having to remove the 54mm (2¼in) high figures from the box.

ABOVE

Ron Wall of St Louis, Missouri, specializes in New Toy Soldiers of the North American Indian wars. The Indian brave, which is just over 54mm (2¼in) in height, has a removable lance.

US PRODUCTION

Among the best-known producers of New Toy Soldiers in the USA are Somerset, Bill Hocker, Edward Burley, Joe Shimek and Stephen Dietz.

Perhaps the most famous range of New Toy Soldiers comes from William Hocker of California. His commitment, eye for detail and exquisite design and manufacturing techniques produce a world-famous product, which comes as close to old hollow-cast figures as can be achieved. These, with many of the superb designs created by companies such as Trophy and Ducal, must be the toy soldier investments of the future.

OTHER PRODUCERS

Imperial of New Zealand, which exports to the USA via Stone Castle Miniatures, is fast making a name in the hobby. Europe has been slower to take up the challenge, with only Italy and Holland daring to break with the tradition of existing and New Antique toy soldiers. Luigi and Monica Toiati of Rome are instrumental in flying the New Soldier flag in Italy under the tradename Garibaldi, and Moorvale Models of the Netherlands under the directorship of Henk Boonstra, is also experimenting with New Toy Soldiers.

CHAPTER SEVEN

NEW METAL MODELS

Britains New Metal Models arrived on the toy soldier scene in 1973, the same year as New Toy Soldiers, but they are quite different. First, although they started at roughly the same time, New Toy Soldiers took off and established themselves much more quickly than did Britains New Metal Models. Second, the method of manufacture is different. New Toy Soldiers are made of white metal alloy sculptured and produced from rubber moulds, usually by way of a centrifugal casting machine. The New Metal Models require the manufacture of a metal die to facilitate the die-cast process. Britains New Metal Models are also slightly larger than the conventional 54mm (2¼in) toy soldier, partly because of the rather thick green metal base on which each figure stands.

From rather tentative beginnings, Britains has, since 1973, recaptured a large slice of the international toy soldier market. The initial issue of the Scots Guard marching figure in 1973 was the start of what has become a somewhat prolific range of figures.

In 1974 two further individual items were produced to accompany the first Scots Guard. These new figures were a Yeoman of the Guard and a Life Guard, which were sold on backing cards and were obviously an attempt to break into the London tourist market. In 1975 six figures were offered in cellophane-fronted boxes, but there followed a curious period of

ABOVE
Britains New Metal Models, packaged in a perspex display box and 54mm (2¼in) high, include a Yeoman of the Guard, a Scots Guard and a Horse Guard together with a sentry box. These figures are available at most of London's major tourist attractions.

inactivity, and only these same three figures were available for the next seven years, although the Guard was used from time to time as a promotional figure for various companies that wanted to provide customers with gifts advertising non-related products.

The first of what became known as Britains Limited Editions was produced in 1983 and marketed in the US through the company's US distributors, Reeves International. Set no. 5183, the Cameron Highlanders, consisted of eleven men and one officer in a red box, and included a certificate verifying the limited availability. The suffix on the set number indicated the year of issue to the collector. This set was exclusive to the USA at a price of $69; it now commands a price of up to $800. The initial range was extended in a small way by giving a different paint style to the foot Life Guard and by the issue of a Horse Guard version. Black Watch and Gordon Highlanders were introduced using a similar

ABOVE
Since the introduction of set no. 1, the Life Guards, Britains has issued updated versions of the regiment's uniforms. The hollow-cast version from the 1950s and the New Metal Model version (top left and right) were joined in 1994 by a boxed set containing examples of the 2nd Life Guards (bottom). This completed 101 years of toy soldier production. All stand 90mm (3½in) high.

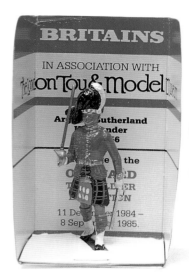

LEFT
Special Britains issues that are not included in the normal catalogue range are sometimes available. These examples of an Argyll and Sutherland Highlander officer and man were available only for the duration of an exhibition held at the London Toy and Model Museum in 1984. The 54mm (2¼in) high figures, which were adapted and painted in the regimental uniform of the Argylls from a standard Britains Highlander, are now quite rare.

RIGHT
These drummers and buglers of the US Marine Corps in summer dress, from the William Britain Collection, are displayed in a perspex presentation box. They stand 54mm (2¼in) high.

casting to that of the Cameron Highlanders. These sets were issued in picture-window boxes and in unlimited quantities.

Mounted Life Guards and Horse Guards were brought out in 1984, again in window boxes. At the same time the second limited edition set, this time for the home market and depicting Mounted Life Guards, set no. 5184, was produced. An exhibition at the London Toy and Model Museum entitled "On Guard" prompted Britains to issue two figures, an officer and a man of the Argyle and Sutherland Highlanders packed on an open-fronted card and available for the duration of the exhibition. Both are now much sought after by collectors.

The investment potential of Britains limited edition sets varies according to the number of sets issued. The 1983 US issue was limited to 3,000 sets. The first UK issue in 1984 was of 7,000 and in 1985 5,000 sets of the Seaforth Highlanders, set no. 5185, were

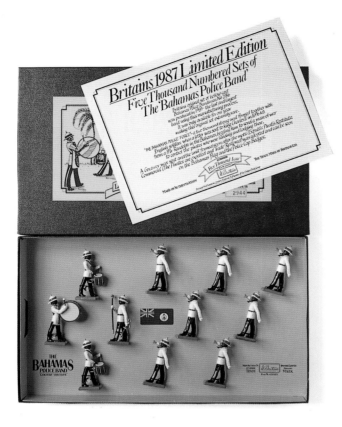

Britains issued this limited edition of the Bahamas Police Band, previously produced in hollow-cast form, in 1987. The certificate issued with each is shown next to the set, and the figures are 54mm (2¼in) high.

ABOVE
A New Metal Model of a Royal Canadian Mounted Policeman. The Mounties, 90mm (3½in) high, have always been popular subjects with Britains, and there have been hollow-cast and plastic versions as well as their inclusion in the Deetail range.

released. 1985 saw the issue of pipers from various Highland regiments together with a mounted model of a Royal Canadian Mounted Policeman, which was an obvious attempt to capture souvenir sales in Canada and so repeat the company's former marketing strategy in that country.

Her Majesty Queen Elizabeth II on horseback, in the uniform of Colonel-in-Chief as worn at the Trooping the Colour ceremony each June in London, was released in 1985 in a cellophane-fronted window box. In 1986 the Household Cavalry range was extended with the introduction of a farrier, standard bearer and trumpeters from both regiments. A London policeman was now included in the London souvenir sets. The limited edition of 5,000 that appeared in 1986 was of the Welsh Guards with flags, and to enhance US sales three sets of US Marine Corps figures were also released. The Trooping the Colour ceremony came to life in a special set issued in 1987 in the form of a book, which opened to reveal the Queen and a representative array of guardsmen present at the ceremony. The same year also saw a Bahamas Police Band in a limited edition of 5,000, while the US Marine Corps range was extended to include bandsmen, guards, drummers and buglers.

The US Marine Corps and guards regiments were further enhanced in 1988 by the production of colour parties, and a set of Royal Marines was brought out, together with Seaforth

Both Harrods and Hamleys, the famous London stores, commissioned Britains to issue various combinations of toy soldiers in special packaging to advertise their shops. The Harrods London set contained a selection of the troops found performing ceremonial duties in the capital together with a figure of HM The Queen on horseback in the uniform worn for Trooping the Colour. The unique packaging stimulated interest in boxes of this kind among collectors. The figures stand 54mm (2¼in) high.

The William Britain limited edition set of the Royal Regiment of Fusiliers, 54mm (2¼in) high, is one of a number of sets to include a regimental mascot. The same set was presented as a prize to celebrate Britains' centenary year at the British Toy Soldier and Figure Show, which was held in June 1993.

Highlanders in tropical uniform, this time in a limited edition of 7,000 sets.

A great deal of repackaging of existing ranges occurred in 1989, and the Middlesex Regiment was the only addition to the standard range. However, the company appears to have recognized the potential of the limited edition range, and two different limited sets were issued – the 22nd Cheshire Regiment and the Royal Marines in tropical dress, both sets restricted to 7,000 each. The practice of issuing two different limited edition sets has continued.

Harrods and Hamleys, the famous London stores, negotiated with Britains to supply Britains soldiers in special boxes with the store's name embossed on them to advertise their respective retail outlets. Although they are not included in Britains catalogues, these sets will undoubtedly increase in value as years progress.

Britains, or Britains Petite, as the company had come to be known, seemed more than ever to be increasing its production and its imaginative approach to toy soldiers. The William Britain range became the new sales name, and it was obvious that Britains Petite was gearing up towards a celebration of 100 years of toy soldier production. The next four years saw many advances, as well as a change of location from London to Nottingham in 1992. As well as the obligatory limited editions, this time 6,000 sets of the

ABOVE AND RIGHT
In the 1990s Britains reverted to the traditional method of packaging: the famous red boxes with illustrated descriptive labels were reintroduced, and the company released toy soldiers in the style of the old hollow-cast figures. Shown here are the Royal Marine Artillery and the Duke of Cambridge's Own 17th Lancers, 90mm (3½in) and 54mm (2¼in) high respectively.

Parachute Regiment, which, for the first time, featured a Mascot in the shape of Pegasus the Shetland pony with the rank of sergeant, and 7,000 sets of the Royal Scots Dragoon Guards, Britains returned to the traditional red boxes for its sets of Coldstream Guards, Worcestershire Regiment and British Infantry in battledress.

The production of boxed sets continued to expand, the contents varying in 1991 to include 17th Lancers and 21st Lancers together with Irish Guards and Somerset Light Infantry. Limited editions were also varied, the quantities different for each of three sets. The US Army Band was intended as an exclusive USA release, and panic buying in the UK pushed up the price to astronomical sums when this was announced; however, many of the 5,000 sets were

ABOVE

Figures personally selected by L.D. Britain, the surviving member of the company founder's family, were brought together and packaged in a two-tier box with a lift-out tray, for issue during the centenary year. The set appeared a year after its intended release. The figures stand 54mm (2¼in) and 90mm (3½in) high.

ABOVE

In addition to limited editions, Britains Petite from time to time issues special figures as commissions from various organizations. This King's Own Scottish Border Piper, 54mm (2¼in) high, was produced in 1992 for the British Toy Retailers' Association and was limited to 1,000 boxes.

returned unsold from the US, thus providing an excess in the UK and a fall in price. The Royal Welsh Fusiliers and the Honourable Artillery Company, in sets of 6,000 and 7,000 respectively, completed the year's releases.

In 1992 small boxes holding either one mounted figure or two foot figures were issued, signalling a return in part to the 1959 system used for the Picture Pack series of hollow-cast toy soldiers. The limited editions were of the Royal Irish Rangers and the 9th/12th Lancers, both in sets of 5,000, and the King's Own Border Regiment, in 6,000 sets. Five new sets in red boxes were introduced, including the Royal Marine Light Infantry and the Middlesex Yeomanry. A different style of packaging, grey boxes with lids, was used for 10 figures, but this venture was short-lived.

The Dennis Britain Set, the subject matter and content of which was chosen by the surviving member of the Britain family, was planned for release in 1992 but did not appear until 1993. It contained a selection of foot soldiers of fusilier regiments and hussars from cavalry regiments, in a two-tier box, designed to commemorate the centenary of the company.

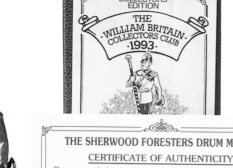

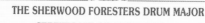

LEFT

The William Britain Collectors Club was started in the company's centenary year, 1993. In addition to a magazine and membership card, members of the Club receive a special figure each year, which make up into a full band. These 54mm (2¼in) high figures, depicting the Sherwood Foresters, are not on general sale, and they are almost certain to become the collectors' items of the future.

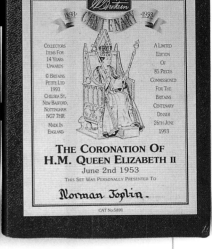

ABOVE

The "Grey boxes", as they have become known, were used for a number of famous regiments. The 54mm (2¼in) high toy soldiers fitted into slots, similar to those in the limited edition boxes, which enabled them to be lifted out and replaced in the groove of the box. The example illustrated is the drums and bugles, with escorts and standards of the Green Howards.

ABOVE

No toy soldiers that were commercially produced can be regarded as unique. However, this 60mm (2⅜in) high model of HM Queen Elizabeth II, issued to commemorate both the 40th anniversary of her accession to the throne and the centenary of Britains Ltd, must be classed as very rare. Each box is inscribed with the name of the owner, and only 85 were produced as gifts to the assembled company attending the Britains centenary dinner in 1993.

The official centenary year was 1993, and three special sets were issued for sale only during the centenary year. There were the Royal Horse Artillery Gun Team, and a Life Guard of 1837 and a Fort Henry Pioneer, both in individual boxes. Limited editions of 4,000 sets of the Royal Regiment of Fusiliers and 5,000 sets of the Band of the Blues and Royals, oddly enough without a bandmaster, were issued, along with the 5th Dragoon Guards and the King's Royal Rifle Corps, in red boxes.

CHAPTER EIGHT

OTHER MATERIALS

Miniature reproductions of soldiers can be found in all sorts of materials from ceramic and porcelain to glass, wood, resin, tin, celluloid and even soap. These items can vary tremendously in size but do not fall within the realms of the collectible toy soldiers discussed in this book. Even aluminium and paper soldiers have not really gained popularity and are not a major part of the hobby. This is perhaps because there is not a sufficient range of items available to fulfil a collector's needs. However, it is worth mentioning them briefly, as at some point most collectors will come across them and they can form a pleasing addition to a collection.

·········· ALUMINIUM ··········

This is perhaps the material most overlooked by collectors. Most of the aluminium figures were produced in France during the 1930s, although some were produced by the firm Wend-An in the UK later on. The method of production was developed by the French firm Quiralu just before World War II. A sand-based moulding tray in two halves was used to convert the aluminium into a toy soldier although the process resulted in a much cruder casting than those for lead figures.

LEFT
Krolyn of Copenhagen made this aluminium Robin Hood, mounted on prancing horse with sword and hunting horn, just prior to World War II. It is 110mm (4½in) high.

BELOW
This boxed set of aluminium Toytown figures were made by Wend-Al. The contents are based on children dressed in Napoleonic military uniforms, and the set includes a rocking horse, nurse and Toytown trees, all 54mm (2¼in) high. It was made in the UK in the 1950s from moulds acquired from the French company, Quiralu.

LEFT
Marx made tinplate toy soldiers in the USA. The 50mm (2in) high figures were meant to be included in shooting games along with a pop gun, and they can form an alternative toy soldier collection.

ABOVE
This unusual 70mm (2¾in) high Highlander is of unknown origin, although it may be German. It was made of celluloid.

Aluminium soldiers were described as unbreakable and they were certainly more resilient than their lead counterparts. The transitional period between lead and plastic gave the aluminium producers a sales opportunity. However they never really became popular and were soon superseded by plastic models. Quiralu became Quiralux and turned to plastic production, selling their moulds and rights to Wend-An, which used the trade name Wend-Al, in the early 1950s.

Aluminium soldiers do not have the same amount of fine detail as those on lead soldiers, due to the softer-style casting process. Paint tends to chip off them more easily than from other types of soldier and the bases on the figures are thick, giving them a clumsy appearance. Although perhaps not part of the mainstream toy soldier hobby, there are small groups of collectors in France and the UK who are beginning to realize the potential of aluminium as a basis for a collection. This has become evident in the bidding at auctions where aluminium soldiers are for sale.

PAPER

Paper toy soldiers were made in the USA by Parker Brothers, Milton Bradley and McLoughlin, usually as part of shooting games. Paper or cardboard toy soldiers were fitted with a wooden block base so that the soldiers could be slotted into the base. These games were supplied with cannons or pop guns to enable the soldiers to be shot at. Understandably, many did not survive. These are not really major collectors' items as toy soldiers but tend to form parts of collections of children's games and toys.

WOOD

Wooden soldiers are in existence – these are really toys – but wood was also an obvious choice for the construction of toy forts. Manufacturers of toy forts often cooperated with toy soldier manufacturers so that the forts would be the right size for the soldiers and so on. Forts can be collectors' items in their own right, but they are bulky and require great areas of space. They compliment a collection of toy soldiers very nicely.

ABOVE
Renee North made these flat plywood figures, 100mm (4in) high, c.1971. They were sold after Mr North's death by long-established toy soldier dealer Shamus Wade, who runs the Commonwealth Forces History Trust Charity.

RIGHT
This wooden toy fort is built in three sections so that it folds up into a box. It was made around 1952 by Cee Bee. It is about 60cm (2ft) in height.

LEFT
This US-made paper soldier, which is 100mm (4in) high, would have formed part of a shooting game, using cardboard and paper soldiers on wooden boxes. It probably dates from 1920.

CHAPTER NINE

SOUVENIRS AND MEMORABILIA

T he words "toy soldier" at first conjure up the idea that they are playthings for children. As tastes change and toy soldiers of different materials have become antiques and collectibles in their own right, they have come to appeal more to adults, and nostalgia or investment are important factors for the adults who collect them.

Toy soldiers sold as souvenirs in gift shops at airports, stately homes or tourist spots are, somewhat surprisingly, becoming collectible, and the Canadian market perhaps reflects this more than any other country in the world. The military-style uniform of the Royal Canadian Mounted Police is recognized by all who are interested in soldiers, and toy soldier manufacturers across the world have capitalized on the Canadian tourist market and produced figures of the famous "Mountie" in all shapes and sizes and in various materials. Gift shops in the Niagara Falls area of Canada are crammed with examples of figures, fridge magnets and snow scenes.

RIGHT
Each Christmas Dorset Soldiers produces a novelty figure for its customers. This guard dog was one of the characters produced in a **limited edition combining military and comic subjects. The series also includes Life Guard, Gnomeguard and Guardian Angel. It is 45mm (1¾in) high.**

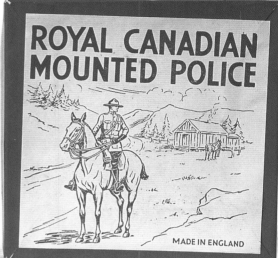

ABOVE
Made in Hong Kong, this antimony lead souvenir item of a West Point Cadet was sold at gift shops near the Academy in New York in the late 1950s. It is 60mm (2⅜in) in height.

ABOVE
Crescent produced this Royal Canadian Mounted Policeman and issued it both as a single piece and in display boxes with other foot figures. This is a rare, individually boxed example produced for export to Canada to celebrate the Canadian centennial in 1967. It was probably one of the last hollow-cast figures made by Crescent and is 90mm (3½in) high.

ABOVE
Souvenir figures that eventually become memorabilia are gaining in popularity. This rocking horse was made for the British Toy Soldier and Figure Show in 1992 and was issued in an illustrated box. It has already become a collector's item because only a limited number were available at the time. It is 90mm (3½in) high.

West Point Academy, New York, has also been a target of attention, with thousands of visitors each year descending on the area, and toy West Point Cadets are readily available. In Greece the famous Evzone or Royal Guard with their unusual, colourful uniforms are an attractive proposition. Scotland, whose tourist industry must be one of the world's largest, is well supplied with Highlanders.

Toy shows also provide the toy soldier collector with a further chance to enhance a collection with souvenir badges or commemorative toy soldiers to bring back fond memories of an enjoyable day. This kind of merchandise is creating a new area of collecting, and sentimental collectors are now willing to pay inflated sums to acquire an item that celebrates a particular show.

CHAPTER TEN

COLLECTING, CARE AND STORAGE

The reasons why people collect toy soldiers are manifold. Many people collect for nostalgic reasons, wanting reminders of childhood toys which have long since disappeared; other people have a fascination for a particular type of soldier; for others it may be an extension of a general interest in things military; still others may enjoy collecting so that they can build up and manoeuvre entire armies; and of course some people see it as a financial investment although this reason is rarely the primary one which inspires a collector.

LEFT
Several manufacturers produced souvenirs for visitors to Fort William Henry in Canada. This rare guard, which is 70mm (2¾in) high, was made by Minikins in Japan in 1950.

ABOVE
Herald plastic figures were made in Hong Kong for a time. These two medieval archers, 54mm (2¼in) and 45mm (1¾in) high, are examples of the cheaper end of Britains' range, manufactured and shipped to the UK from the company's subsidiary in Hong Kong in the 1970s.

Collecting became fashionable in the early 1960s as lead toy soldiers were going out of production. As ranges and lines were discontinued, so collectors began to acquire them, realizing that they would no longer be available through the usual retail outlets. Since then the hobby has grown to embrace more and more people.

·········· FOCUSING A COLLECTION ··········

What kind of soldiers you decide to collect is very much a matter of personal preference. However, there are some general factors which are useful to bear in mind before you get started as they will help you to decide what direction you want your collection to go in and to make sure that you get maximum satisfaction from it.

The first question to ask yourself is what you are particularly interested in. Do you have a special area you want to focus on? Perhaps you will want to collect a particular type of soldier, or the work of a particular manufacturer. Collections can be arranged by manufacturer, size, type of material or you can concentrate on certain periods in history, individual wars and campaigns, types of uniform or even particular regiments. It may be that at the beginning your collection will contain a mixture of items and as you become more involved in the hobby you will decide how you want to specialize.

Another factor to bear in mind early on is cost. Some soldiers are much more expensive than others and you need to be able to assess which areas of collecting suit your pocket as well as your taste. If you are intent on putting together an entire army or simply want to amass a huge collection of as many toy soldiers as you can lay your hands on, bear in mind the probable cost!

It is useful to scout around the various toy soldier outlets if you are a newcomer to the hobby. This will give you an idea of what is available and what the prices are before you commit yourself to a purchase.

Collecting toy soldiers has never been easier than it is currently. As the hobby has grown, specialist shops have sprung up and you will find one in most of the world's major cities. In addition to these, soldiers are commonly available from toy shows, flea markets, antique fairs and markets and at auctions. Then there is always the chance that you will find something special at a car boot sale, jumble sale or in a junk shop. Swapmeets are also popular where you can meet with other enthusiasts and swap items.

· GUIDE TO AUCTION PROCEDURES ·

Auctions deserve a special mention. They are a good source of toy soldiers but can be daunting. Attending auctions can be both a source of revenue (if you are selling) or an opportunity to purchase toy soldiers either as single pieces or in multiple lots. They also provide an opportunity to see what is on the market and what the prices are. There are several basic rules that will make the purchase of toy soldiers more enjoyable.

1. Make yourself aware of each individual auction house's rules, commission rate and VAT on commission.

2. Remember that the "hammer price" will, in most cases, be subject to a basic percentage rate of auctioneer's commission and in some cases, usually indicated in the catalogue, a VAT charge.

3. If possible obtain a catalogue in advance and try to view the items you wish to purchase.

4. If you are selling at auction take into account the auction house commission rules, as this will be deducted from the price that your item realizes.

5. Consult the auction house regarding reserves for your items to ensure that if your property does not reach the expected price level it will not be sold for less than your agreed reserve.

IDENTIFICATION OF TOY
······························ SOLDIERS ·······························

The majority of toy soldiers bear some mark on the underside of the base which is sometimes only the country of manufacture. Others have the name of the manufacturer or are marked in a way that gives an indication of its origin.

John Hill marked "Johillo" or "John Hill" on their figures but

ABOVE
Britains issued a series of large Scottish clansmen in the 1980s, which were contained in a perspex box. The figures, 100mm (4in) high, are more akin to statuettes than toy soldiers, and they are sold through gift and souvenir outlets.

ABOVE
John Hill & Co. was not successful when it came to producing plastic figures. This clansman, issued under the Monarch label, is one of only a few sets made during the late 1950s and is 54mm (2¼in) high.

also stamped on an abbreviation of "copyright", spelt "copyrt".

Britains marked nearly every figure, but used a variety of marks including their name, Britains Ltd. Only very early examples may not carry a mark. For a while the company used paper labels until all their moulds could be retooled to accommodate the copyright stamp. These paper labels are not always in place which may be confusing for the novice collector.

Items found in their original boxes provide obvious evidence of the manufacturer. If you can get hold of original or reproduction catalogues this can also help with identification. There are a number of books dealing with the subject of identification (see *Further Reading*, page 77) and the inexperienced collector will find these references very useful.

···· DISPLAYING YOUR COLLECTION ····

Part of the pleasure of having a collection of toy soldiers is being able to enjoy looking at them. The most popular method of displaying them is in cases or on shelves (it helps if these are enclosed so that dust does not become a problem but air should be allowed to circulate round the items). The collector will decide which soldiers they want to display together, according to size, regiments and so on. Individual soldiers can be displayed singly.

Some collectors prefer to arrange their figures so that they form a scene or diorama, perhaps depicting a real or imaginary reconstruction of a state occasion, battle or historical incident.

················ STORAGE AND CARE ················

Those unable to display their collections should ensure that lead soldiers are stored in a dry and well-ventilated area in strong cardboard boxes with a light covering of tissue paper. Plastic figures tend to become brittle and they should only be stored in a single row with no pressure being put on them.

A word needs to be said about lead rot, sometimes called lead

ABOVE
There were many makers of hollow-cast figures in France. Mignot, better known for its solid items, made some hollow-cast soldiers, but little research has been carried out into the other firms producing hollow-cast pieces.

The bases of some of them are marked with various initials, including LP and GM, but these firms defy identification. French manufacturers of hollow-cast figures tended to portray French soldiers in toy form. The Mameluke in a turban, 54mm (2¼in) in height,

is from the Napoleonic era, as are the two old guard troops, 54mm (2¼in), with large heads, which give them a toy-like appearance. The 54mm (2¼in) high British Tommy, throwing a grenade, is unusual because the subject area was rarely covered in France.

RIGHT
This 50mm (2in) high plastic Saracen with a spear was previously made by Charbens in lead from a hollow-cast mould.

disease, which can appear in lead toy soldiers. Much research has been carried out into the causes of this, without any real conclusions being drawn. It is possible that certain methods of manufacture may encourage lead rot. It is known that storage in damp conditions does not help and it has also been proved that direct contact with oak wood can be a contributory factor. Display or storage in airtight conditions is to be avoided.

The signs to watch out for are a grey powdering of the lead. As soon as you spot this, isolate the item from the others in your collection in case they also become affected.

REPAIR, RESTORATION AND CONVERSIONS

A growing number of collectors are trying to obtain broken or damaged toy soldiers, as their special interest is in repairing old toy soldiers to restore them to their former glory. Other people obtain broken or even complete toy soldiers and convert them into something else. They may put together pieces from two or more incomplete soldiers to make a whole one.

Repainting, converting, repairing and restoring toy soldiers for your own pleasure is a very worthwhile exercise. However, it adds nothing to the value and most collectors who do not wish to do this look for figures that are in good condition.

VALUE

If a figure is in good condition when you buy it and remains so, the likelihood is that its value will remain firm or will even increase with age. Repainting, converting and repairing tend to devalue figures, so remember this if you want to resell items.

For those who are interested in investment, it is a very good idea to keep an inventory of your collection. Make a note of the price you paid originally for each item and from time to time find out from toy soldier dealers what it is currently worth. This means that you can keep a running record of what your collection is worth, which is useful for insurance purposes as well as being interesting.

ABOVE
This splendid casting in plastic of a Roman legionnaire mounted on a galloping horse was one of a series made in Germany during the 1960s and 1970s by Hausser. It is 100mm (4in) high and has a detachable rider.

CHAPTER ELEVEN

TOY SOLDIER
SHOWS AND AUCTIONS

S H O W S

The first thematic Toy Soldier Show was held in Chicago in 1979. It was organized in conjunction with the then Old Toy Soldier Newsletter, and Don Pielin set out to prove that the readers of the publication, together with dealers and collectors, would attend a show devoted to toy soldiers and figures, for until then toy shows were events at which general toy merchandise was on sale. From humble beginnings, it has turned into the largest of its kind in the world. Other shows have emerged – Kulmbach in Germany and the East and West Coast shows in the USA, together with Valley Forge in Pennsylvania – but none can compare with the 280-table Old Toy Soldier Show in Chicago each September. Just about every type of toy soldier ever produced has been and can be found at this show, with dealers arriving in the Hyatt Hotel as early as the previous Friday to trade and prepare for the following Sunday. It has been likened to a toy soldier collectors' paradise and has served to promote the toy soldier collecting hobby worldwide.

Norman and Sheila Joplin organized the first major Toy Soldier Show in the UK in 1991. The British Toy Soldier and Figure Show is now Europe's largest event and is supported by their American counterparts from Chicago. It is held twice each year at the Royal

A B O V E

Tin or enamel badges issued at toy soldier shows have joined the ranks of collectible items, perhaps serving to remind the collector of a day spent seeking that elusive figure for their collection. The small pin is a US item from the Chicago Old Toy Soldier Show, issued to commemorate its 10th anniversary.

National Hotel, Bedford Way, London, UK, on the last Saturday in June and first Saturday in December.

It is recommended that before travelling to a show you should make contact with the organizers to ensure the event is taking place. Many other shows take place in the USA – only the major events are included here – and for further details of other shows you should consult one of the periodicals listed on page 78.

T O Y   S O L D I E R   S H O W S

Birmingham Model and Toy Soldier Fayre
Held each October. Organizer: David McKenna, 20 Poston Court, Kings Heath, Birmingham B14 5AB, UK.

British Model Soldier Society
National and local branch activities include trade standards. See Societies and Clubs, page 79.

Euro Militaire
A two-day military modelling event held each September at the Leas Cliff Hall, Folkestone, Kent, UK.

Folkestone International Toy Soldier Show
This is held each March at the Metropole Suite, Folkestone, Kent, UK.

Soldiers and Figure Show
Held each February at the Gloucester Leisure Centre. Organizer: Lilliane Tunstill, 110/112 Bath Road, Cheltenham, Gloucestershire, UK.

UK Toy and Model Soldier Show
Organized by *Plastic Warrior* and held each May at the Queen Charlotte Hall, Parkshot, Richmond, Surrey, UK.

Old Toy Soldier Show, Chicago
Held each September at the Hyatt Regency, Woodfield, Schaumburg, Illinois. Organized in conjunction with *Old Toy Soldier* magazine. Contact: Don Pielin, 1009 Kenilworth, Wheeling, Illinois, USA.

Toronto Old Soldier Sale
Held each October at the Regal Constellation Hotel, 900 Dixon Road, Toronto, Canada. Organizer: Stewart Saxe.

Annual East Coast Toy Soldier Show and Sale
Held each November at the Fairleigh Dickinson University, Hackensack, New Jersey, USA, and run in conjunction with *Toy Soldier Review* magazine. Contact: Bill Lango.

The Camileri Westchester Toy Soldier Show
Held each November at the Westchester County Centre, White Plains, New York, USA. Contact: Frank Fusco.

West Coaster Toy Soldier Show
Held each March at the Inn at The Park Hotel, 1855 South Harbor Boulevard, Anaheim, California 92802, USA. Contact: Bob Fisher.

MFCA (Miniature Figure Collectors of America) Annual Show and Exhibition
Held each May at Valley Forge Convention Centre, King of Prussia, Pennsylvania, USA. Contact: Alban Shaw.

Hobby Militaire of the Ontario Model Soldier Society
Held each June at the Novotel North York, 3 Park Home Avenue, North York, Toronto, Canada. Contact: Ted Kennedy.

Annapolis Toy Soldier Show
Held each July at the Annapolis Hotel, Annapolis, Maryland, USA. Contact: Dick Sossi.

Indiana Toy Soldier Show
Held each March at the Ramada Inn, 7701 42nd Street, Indianapolis, Indiana, USA. Contact: Barry Carter.

North East Toy Soldier Society Soldier Show
Held each April at Dedham, Massachusetts, USA. Contact: Dick Charlesworth, 121 Cherry Brook Road, Weston, MA 02193, USA.

Long Island Toy Soldier Show
Held each September at Elks Lodge, 57 Hempstead Avenue, Lynbrook, Long Island, New York, USA. Contact: Vinny Pugliese.

Kulmbach Deutschen und Internationale Zinnfiguren Borse Show
Held in August on alternate years at Kulmbach, Bavaria. Details from German Tourist Information.

AUCTIONS

The following auction houses hold either specialist toy soldier auctions or regularly include sections devoted to the sale of toy soldiers within their regular toy sales. In addition to the following, collectors may often find that local or provincial auction houses include toy soldiers in their antique auctions.

AUCTIONS

Christies, South Kensington Ltd. Contact: Hugo Marsh or Daniel Agnew, 85 Old Brompton Road, London SW7 3LD, UK.

Lacy Scott, 10 Risbygate Street, Bury St Edmunds, Suffolk, UK. Contact: George Beevis or Peter Crichton.

Phillips Bayswater, 10 Salem Road, Bayswater, London W2 4DL, UK. Contact: James Opie (consultant).

Wallis & Wallis, West Street Auction Galleries, Lewes, Sussex BN7 2NJ, UK. Contact: Glen Butler.

Henry Kurtz Ltd, 163 Amsterdam Avenue, Suite 136, New York, New York, USA 10023.

BELOW
Auction catalogues can form a useful library, which can be referred to before forthcoming auctions. If you attend the auction, make a note of the prices for each lot, which can help when you are bidding in the future.

LEFT
Cavendish Miniatures started to produce plastic figures in the early 1950s and is still in business, operating from Windsor in the UK. This box of 1750 infantry, all 54mm (2¼in) high, is one of its early sets, and forms part of a range issued continuously since 1958.

FURTHER READING

Asquith, Stuart, *The Collector's Guide to New Toy Soldiers*, Argus Books, Hemel Hempstead, 1991

Carman, W.Y., *Model Soldiers*, Charles Letts & Co., London, 1973

Fontana, Dennis, *The War Toys 2: The Story of Lineol*, New Cavendish Books, London, 1991

Garratt, John G., *Model Soldiers: A Collector's Guide*, Seeley Services, London, 1965

Garratt, John G., *Collecting Model Soldiers*, David & Charles, Newton Abbot, 1975

Garratt, John G., *The World Encyclopedia of Model Soldiers*, Frederick Muller, London, 1981

Greenhill, Peter, *Heraldic Miniature Knights*, Guild of Master Craftsmen, 1991

Johnson, Peter, *Toy Armies*, B.T. Batsford, London, 1981

Joplin, Norman, *British Toy Figures 1900–Present*, Arm & Armour Press, London, 1987

Joplin, Norman, *The Great Book of Hollow-cast Figures*, New Cavendish Books, London, 1993

Kearton, George, *The Collector's Guide to Plastic Toy Soldiers*, Ross Anderson Publications, 1987

Kurtz, Henry L. and Ehrlich, Burtt, *The Art of the Toy Soldier*, New Cavendish Books, London, 1979

London Toy and Model Museum, *On Guard* (catalogue of exhibition), New Cavendish Books, London, 1984

McKenzie, Ian, *Collecting Old Toy Soldiers*, B.T. Batsford, London, 1975

Nevins, Edward, *Forces of the British Empire 1914*, Vandamere Press, 1993

O'Brien, Richard, *Collecting Toy Soldiers no. 1*, Books Americana, 1990

O'Brien, Richard, *Collecting Toy Soldiers, no. 2*, Books Americana, 1992

Opie, James, *Britains Toy Soldiers 1893–1932*, Gollancz, London, 1985

Opie, James, *British Toy Soldiers 1893 to the Present*, Arms & Armour Press, London, 1985

Opie, James, *Phillips Collectors' Guides: Toy Soldiers*, Boxtree, London, 1989

Opie, James, *Collecting Toy Soldiers*, New Cavendish Books, London, 1992

Opie, James, *The Great Book of Britains*, New Cavendish Books, London, 1993

Pielin, Don, *American Dimestore Soldiers*, private publication, 1975

Polaine, Reggie and Halkins, David, *The War Toys 1: The Story of Hausser-Elastolin* (2nd edition), New Cavendish Books, London, 1991

Richards, L.W., *Old British Model Soldiers 1893–1918*, Arms & Armour Press, London, 1970

Roer, Hans H., *Old German Toy Soldiers*, private publication, 1993

Rose, Andrew, *The Collector's All-colour Guide to Toy Soldiers*, Salamander, London, 1985

Ruddle, John, *Collector's Guide to Britains Model Soldiers*, Model & Allied Publications, 1980

Wallis, Joe, *Regiments of All Nations*, private publication, 1981

Wallis, Joe, *Armies of the World*, private publication, 1983

RIGHT

This nurse with an ether bottle and mask, 65mm (2½in) high, was manufactured by Eccles Brothers of Iowa. The company acquired the original dimestore mould, which had never been used, and this figure is, therefore, not a reproduction but a modern casting made from an old mould.

PERIODICALS

The following periodicals contain information about, and articles on, toy soldiers and toy soldier collecting.

Les Amis de Starlux

See Societies and Clubs, page 79.

Bulletin

The journal issued by the British Model Soldier Society to members only. See Societies and Clubs, page 79.

Collector's Gazette

A general hobby newspaper, 10 editions each year, including regular features and reports on toy soldier shows and auctions. Contact: 200 Nuncargate Road, Kirby-in-Ashfield, Nottinghamshire NG17 9AG, UK.

Figuren Magazine

The magazine for Germany's toy soldier collectors. Contact: Andreas Pletruschka, Spenerstrasse 17, 1000 Berlin 21, Germany.

Holger Eriksson Collector Society

A quarterly newsletter specializing in the products and associated companies of Eriksson. Contact: Lou Sandbote, 5307E Mockingbird, Suite 802, Dallas, Texas 75206-5109, USA.

Military Hobbies

A bi-monthly magazine, of which a large proportion is devoted to toy soldiers and toy soldier manufacturing products. Contact: Pireme Publishing Ltd, 34 Chatsworth Road, Charminster, Bournemouth BH6 8SW, UK.

Military Modelling

Includes a monthly soldier box column giving details of toy soldier products and events. Contact: Argus Specialist Publications, Argus House, Boundary Way, Hemel Hempstead HP2 7ST, UK.

Old Toy Soldier Newsletter

A bi-monthly publication covering all aspects of old and new toy soldier collecting. Contact: Steve and Josie Sommers (editors), 209 North Lombard, Oak Park, Illinois 60302-2503, USA.

Plastic Figures and Playset Collector

Specializes in plastic figures produced by Marx. Contact: Tom Terry (editor), PO Box 1355, La Crosse, Wisconsin 54602-1355, USA.

ABOVE
A variety of toy soldier hobby magazines are published. All of them contain useful information on where to obtain toy soldiers as well as advertisements for companies that make or supply new and old toy soldiers and figures.

The Plastic Warrior

Magazine, available by subscription, for collectors interested in and specializing in collecting plastic toy soldiers. Contact: 65 Walton Court, Woking, Surrey GU21 5EE, UK.

Toy Soldier Review

A quarterly publication covering old and new toy soldiers. Contact: Bill Lango (editor), c/o Vintage Castings, 127 74th Street, North Bergen, New Jersey 07047, USA.

The William Britain

The magazine of the William Britain Collectors Club. See Societies and Clubs, page 79.

Woody's Word

A quarterly newsletter covering toy soldier news and events. Contact: M.D. Paulussen, 19 Seneca Trail, Wayne, New Jersey 07470, USA.

SOCIETIES AND CLUBS

Les Amis de Starlux (The Friends of Starlux)
A regular magazine provides details of Starlux's
products. Details from: Patrice Reynaud, 9 Grand rue,
11400 Ville Neuve, La Comptar, France.

British Model Soldier Society
This long-established society caters for the needs of the
toy and model soldier collector. There are regional
branches, exhibitions and competitions and an annual
national event in London. Part of the society's own
collection is displayed at Hatfield House, Hertfordshire.
Membership details from: Ian R. Webb, Honorary
Treasurer, 35 St John's Road, Chelmsford,
Essex CM2 0TX, UK.

Toy Soldier Collectors of America
A directory of members both in the USA and throughout
the world. Details from: John Giddings, 5340 40th
Avenue North, St Petersburgh, Florida 33709, USA.

William Britain Collectors Club
Membership includes a special Britains figure, issued
each year exclusively to members, who also receive a
twice-yearly magazine and details of forthcoming Britains
figures. Membership details from: William Britain
Collectors Club, PO Box 1946, Halesowen, West
Midlands B63 3TS, UK.

BELOW
**Regular exhibitions of toy soldiers
are held all over the UK and the
USA, and attractive advertising
leaflets are often produced to
promote such ventures. This
advertisement was produced for
an exhibition commemorating the
40th anniversary of the Queen's
accession to the throne, and it
features a reconstruction of the
Coronation procession using toy
soldiers.**

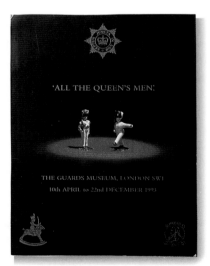

ABOVE
**Books, periodicals and journals for
collectors' clubs are useful
reference material. Illustrated here
are a number of US examples. The
book in the foreground was the
first to attempt to tell the story of
US dimestore figures.**

INDEX

Italic page numbers refer to picture captions.

Abel, C.D., & Co. 17
Aeoha 44
AHI 37
Airfix 34, 42
Albion 50
All Nu 30
aluminium figures 47, 64–5, 64, 65
Alymer 8, 14
American Soldier Company 8, 30
Anglo-Russian Toy Soldier Company 14
Atlantic 47
Auburn 30
auctions 71, 76
Ausley 44
Authenticast 7, 14

B.G. of G.B. 50
badges 74
Baetz, Walter 32
Barclay Manufacturing Company 9, 29, 30–1, 31, 32, 32, 33
Barrett and Sons 33
Bastion 50, 53
Benbros 24, 42, 45
Beton 34, 34, 44
Blenheim 48–9, 49, 52, 53
BMC 22, 23
Boonstra, Henk 55
boxed sets 6, 16, 16, 17, 20, 21, 35, 65, 72
Bracamontes, Ric 47
Brent Toy Company 28
Britain, William, Junior 7, 15, 16
Britains 16–21, 19, 24, 33, 39, 42
    Armies of the World 16, 17
    boxed sets 16, 16, 17, 20, 21, 56, 58, 61–3, 61, 63
    Deetail 9, 38–9, 40, 41, 59
    Dennis Britain Set 62–3, 62
    Eyes Right 19, 37–8, 38, 43
    guns 18, 19
    Herald 19, 36, 37, 38, 70
    Knights of Agincourt 21, 21
    Knights of the Sword 39
    Limited Editions 57–63, 62
    marks and labels 17, 72
    movable and interchangeable parts 37, 38, 39
    New Metal Models 39, 49–50, 56–63, 56–63
    Picture Packs 15, 21
    plastic figures 37–9
    Regiments of All Nations 20, 20
    Scottish clansmen 71
    State Coach 19, 20, 25
    Swoppet 37–8, 38
    William Britain Collectors Club 63
Britains Petite 60
British Bulldog 50
British Model Soldier Society 12
Brown, Giles 53

Campaign 50
caring for collections 72–3
Carman, W.Y. 12
cast iron figures 30, 31, 32
casting sets 32–3
casual poses 7
Cavendish Miniatures 42–3, 76
Cee Bee 66
celluloid figures 64, 65
ceramic and glass figures 64
Charbens 23–4, 41, 42, 43
Cherilea 33, 34, 41–2, 42, 43, 43
cigarette packets 11
Comansi 47
Comet 7, 14
Company B 47
composition figures 8, 8, 26–8, 26–8
connoisseur figures 12, 13, 14
conversions 73
Cowan, Peter 49
Crescent 16, 23, 24, 33, 34–5, 41, 42, 42, 43, 68

Davies 17
detachable pieces 11
die-cast figures 56
dimestore figures 7–8, 8, 9, 25, 25, 29–33, 29–33, 34, 34
display 72
display cards 35
Dorset Soldiers 43, 43, 53, 67, 69
Ducal 51, 53
Durolin 27–8
Durso 27

Eccles Brothers 33, 77
Elastolene 28
Elastolin 26–7, 26, 45–6, 46
Ellis, Michael 45, 45
Empire 50
Eriksson, Holger 7, 14, 34
Eureka 30

Female figures 22, 27, 28, 31, 47, 77
Figur 12, 14
Figur Brevitt 27, 27
flat figures 6–7, 6, 10, 11, 33
focusing a collection 70
Fry, A. 17, 17, 22, 23
Fylde Manufacturing Company 24

Gamage, Arthur 16
Garibaldi 55, 55
Gaugemaster 46
Gemodels 42
GM 25, 25
Greenwood and Ball 9, 13
Grey Iron 29–30, 31, 32
Greys Cigarette Co. 11
Gunner 50
guns 18, 19

Haley, Gerrard 51
Hall, Charles 52
Hamleys 24, 60, 60
Hanks Brothers 17, 17, 22, 23
Harrods 24, 60, 60
Harvey 24
Hausser 26–7, 26, 46, 73
heads, plug-in 10, 11, 11, 12
Heinrichsen 7
Herald 19, 21, 35, 35, 36, 37, 37, 45, 70
Heyde, George 11–12, 11, 13
Hill, John, & Co. 22–3, 22, 23, 24, 33, 35, 71–2, 71
Hocker, Bill 55
hollow-cast figures 7–8, 7, 15–25, 15–25, 30, 34, 37, 48, 72
Hummel 12

Identifying figures 71–2
Imperial 55
injection moulding 8, 34
Insel 14, 14
interchangeable parts 37, 38, 41

Jacklex 50
Jean 45
Johillco see Hill, John, & Co.
Jones, Edward 25, 25, 30

Kelloggs cereal packets 35
Kentoys 42
Kidogo 54
kits 12
Kresge 28, 29
Krolyn 65

Large-scale figures 28
lead figures 6–7, 8–9, 10, 21
lead rot (lead disease) 72–3
Levy, Donze and Michael 30
Lido 44
Lincol 27
Lincoln Logs 8, 30, 30
London Collector's Shop 13
Lone Star 41, 42
LP 25
Lucotte 10

McCrory 29
McLoughlin 30, 66
Macys 33
magazines and periodicals 78
Malleable Mouldings 34, 35
Manoil 29, 31, 32, 32, 33
Mark Time 48, 50
Marksmen 45, 45
Marlborough 43, 52, 53
Marx, Louis, & Co. 44–5, 44, 45, 65
measuring model soldiers 11
Mignot 10–11, 10, 12, 25, 72
military miniatures 12, 13, 14, 14
Militia 50

Miller 28, 28, 30
Milton Bradley 66
Minikins 30, 33, 70
MKL 53
Mode, M.J. 50
Monarch 71
Moorvale Models 55
movable parts 17, 25, 33, 37, 39, 42, 47
Mudie 17

Nardi 47
Neisner 29
New Toy Soldiers 9, 48–55, 48–55, 56
    manufacturers 54
Newberry 29
Newton, Norman 13
North, Renee 66
Northern Toy Soldiers 51
Nostalgia 49, 53

O'Brien, Richard 29

Paper figures 64, 66, 66
papier-mâché 26
Parker Brothers 66
Pfeiffer 26
Pielin, Don 29
plaster figures 28, 28, 30
plastic figures 8, 20, 24, 31, 34–47, 34–47, 70, 71, 76
playsets 44
Playwood Plastics 8, 32
plug-in pieces 10, 11, 11, 12, 13
pod-foot figures 30, 31
Polk's Hobby Stores 14
Poplar Playthings 43
porcelain figures and heads 27, 64

Quiralu 64, 65, 65
Quiralux 47, 65

Reamsa 46–7, 47
Reeves International 57
reissued figures 43, 43, 47
Reka 22, 23
repairs and restoration 73
reproductions and copies 12, 45, 45, 46
resin figures 64
Riviere and Willett 28
Rose, Andrew 49, 50, 51, 53
Rose Miniatures 14
rubber figures 30, 43
Russell Gamage 13

Sachs 33
Sacul 42
Sale 25
Schiercke, Henry 33
Scroby, Frank and Jan 48–50, 52, 53
Sears Roebuck 45
Selwyn Smith, Roy 21, 21, 24, 24

semi-flat figures 7
shows 74–5
slush-cast figures 7–8, 25, 29–33
societies and clubs 79
Soldiers Soldiers 50–1, 50
solid figures 7, 8, 9, 10–14, 10–14
    New Toy Soldiers see New Toy Soldiers
souvenirs and memorabilia 67–8, 67, 68, 70
Speedwell 42
Stadden, Charles 13, 14, 14
Star Collectables 53
Starlux 45, 47
Steadfast 54
Stone Castle Miniatures 55
storage 72–3
Swedish African Engineers 14

Tabony, Martin 53
Taylor, F.G., and Sons 33
Taylor, Len 53
Taylor & Barratt 24
Thompson, Major Gavin 54
Timpo 24, 24, 28, 34, 35, 39, 41, 41, 42, 42, 43
tinplate figures 44, 64, 65
Toiati, Luigi and Monica 55, 55
Tommy Toy 30
Tooth, Norman 41, 42
Toy Importers see Timpo
Toydell 27
Toyway 43
Tradition of London 7, 12
Trafalgar 50
Treasure Chest 12
Trico 33
Trojan 42
Trophy Miniatures 51
Trophy of Wales 50, 53
Tunstill, John 50, 50

Una 42, 45

Valuing collections 73
VP 42, 45

Wade, Shamus 49, 66
Wall, Ron 55
Warren 30
Wend-Al 47, 65, 65
Wend-An 64, 65
Wessex 50
white metal figures 9, 48, 56, 69
Winkler, F. 34
Wood, George 22
wooden figures 64, 66, 66
Woolworths 22, 24, 29, 34

Zang Products 35, 35, 36